THIS

MODERN

MUSIC

Gerald Abraham, G.E.H.

New York

W · W · NORTON & COMPANY · INC ·

FIRST AMERICAN EDITION 1952
COPYRIGHT AS TO REVISIONS BY
W. W. NORTON & COMPANY, INC. 1952

This work under the title *This Modern Stuff*
was published in Great Britain in 1933 and revised in 1939

MANUFACTURED IN THE U.S.A. FOR
THE PUBLISHERS BY THE VAIL-BALLOU PRESS

10/78

THIS

MODERN

MUSIC

CONTENTS

BY WAY OF EXPLANATION

My Dear Con,

Here, in a form which you probably didn't expect, is the answer to your request. It has taken this form because there must be thousands like you in this country alone, devout lovers of the music of the great masters of the past, who are completely bothered by "this modern stuff" but who *want* to understand it. I can't "show you how to appreciate it." No one can. But I have done my best to give you the right clues and set you on the right paths. You must decide for yourself whether the treasure was worth all the trouble when you have found it. You may be inclined to agree with Tony Weller's charity boy when he got to the end of the alphabet—"vether it's vorth goin' through so much to learn so little is a matter o' taste. *I* rayther think it isn't." But you must remember that different people put very different valuations on music which is now everyone's possession. When you understand Bartók as easily as you understand Beethoven, if ever, you may still be as far as you are at present from sharing my opinion of the value of his music.

I have done my best not to overload my explanation with technical terms. But some technical terms you must have. I defy anyone to talk sense, or even plausible nonsense, about a motor car or a baseball game without using technical terms. And it can't be done about music. It is useless to write books for people who are too lazy to pick up a few elementary technicalities about the subject they pretend to be interested in. At the same time I have tried to remember that you didn't get very far with the book I recommended to you in the first place, by far the best book on contemporary music which has yet appeared in the English language —Dyson's *The New Music*. Dyson wrote for people who know their way about the world of music rather better than you do. But go back to him when you've finished this—if you do ever manage to finish it! You may find that some of his rough places—the most interesting bits, mind you—have become smoother.

I have used plenty of musical examples, choosing them wherever possible from piano pieces and piano scores, so that you can get hold of the whole things and see the examples in their proper context. And that, by the way, is your chief sign of grace, the token that you really are musical. I mean the fact that you are not content always to have your music made for you (though made so well, so easily and so cheaply), that quite often your inward demon can be appeased only by your own music-making—too flattering a term (you would say yourself) to apply to what Ruth calls your "appalling strumming." So wait till the rest of the family have gone to the pictures, mislay *The Radio Times*, and have some fun with the piano. And good luck to you.

Yours ever,
G. A.

NOTE TO AMERICAN READERS

THIS little book was originally published in 1933. A good deal can happen in nearly twenty years, and a good deal has happened in music, as well as in world history. The landscape has changed in many details; new figures have appeared and come to the fore-ground. Yet the basic difficulties which stand between the average music-lover and his full appreciation of "modern" music remain unchanged, and I am told that this modest little effort of mine to help him over them is still being found as useful as ever.

9

Now, for this American edition, I have taken the opportunity to add a few more musical examples and to revise some details of the text. And since (as I have said) the world of contemporary music looks a bit different in 1952 from its appearance in 1933, I have added a chapter in which I have tried to show the whole course of events in twentieth-century music in clear perspective.

THIS
MODERN
MUSIC

1

THE NATURE OF THE PROBLEM

WHAT exactly do we mean by "modern music"? Or, to put it another way, when does what we consider modernism in music begin? With *Tristan*, which after all dates back to the Indian Mutiny year? With Debussy, nearly sixty years ago? The *Suite Bergamasque* for piano, the *Prélude à l'Après-midi d'un Faune* and the String Quartet all date from the early nineties, years before the Boer War, yet some of us still count these modern, and there are plenty of people who still find them difficult to listen to—though cultured musicians living in centers of musical activity will find it difficult to believe that. Suppose we draw our line a little nearer the present year. Even *Le Sacre du Printemps* and Schoenberg's *Five Orchestral Pieces* are forty years old; so that, considering the tininess even now of the minority who can accept them as normal music, we must reckon that the musical world as a whole (that vast majority of musicians and music-lovers whose tastes are intelligent without being intellectual) is nearly half a century behind the composers. There is no need to worry about that. It is no very new state of affairs, though the vanguard has probably never got quite so far ahead of the main body as it has recently. And as, during the last few years, the vanguard seems to have got into difficulties through meeting unexpected obstacles and taking a few wrong turnings, the main body has now an excellent opportunity to reduce the gap and re-establish more substantial contact with the pioneers.

Practically, of course, the attempt to define modernism with the help of a time-limit is futile. Leaving aside the numerous contemporary compositions which belong in spirit and letter to the middle of the last century, there are plenty of works genuinely modern in spirit (for instance, Vaughan Williams's *London Symphony*) which cannot present much difficulty— or at most only passing, incidental difficulties—to the ear of any open-minded listener accustomed to the idioms of Wagner, Brahms and their contemporaries. Nor is all the music written by modernist composers "modern" in any real sense. Anyone making the acquaintance of Debussy, Ravel and Sibelius through the

Arabesques, the *Pavane pour une Infante Défunte* or the orchestral *Bolero*, and the *Valse Triste*, might justifiably conclude that the ugliness and "difficulty" of modern music had been terribly over-rated and that these three composers, at any rate, outstanding names among the moderns, are very charming fellows whose music calls for no special effort to understand it. Actually, of course, each of these works is about as characteristic of its composer as *Für Elise* is of the Beethoven of the *Appassionata*, the symphonies and the concertos. It contains just about as much of the composer's real musical self. (By which I don't mean that it contains none of it.) Each might usefully serve as an introduction to its composer's serious work, but only as a sort of cocktail before the meal.

But we must remember that a liking for one or two works like these by modernist composers does not imply ability to appreciate or understand modern music. The string melody in the middle section of *L'Après-midi d'un Faune* is no more modern than Massenet or Gounod. Anyone not tone-deaf must appreciate its luscious sweetness. But whereas at first it may seem the best part of the whole piece and act as the sugar which helps us to swallow the pill, its cloying quality will soon pall on those with natural good taste and as their liking for the rest of the *Prélude* increases they will resent the intrusion of this commonplace idea into the otherwise perfect midsummer afternoon's dream. Such marks of a familiar world, not yet by any means left behind, are naturally helpful and heartening to any rather timid adventurer, but he must be careful not to reason in this way: "This is a modern work. Here in it is something perfectly comprehensible and which I like immensely. Therefore this is *good* modern music, not like the cacophonous rubbish of Bartók and Webern, which is therefore probably *bad*." I am not suggesting, to go to the other extreme, that all the easily comprehensible and immediately attractive elements in modern music are bad or old-fashioned (or both, like the Debussy example), though it is reasonable to suppose that the best modern music, like that of any age, is that which does not yield up all its secrets at the first two or three hearings. All I wish to insist on is that the explorer must be on his guard against accepting fragments of the old which are embedded in modern music, or bear the name of a contemporary composer, as new, and then using these in any way as a standard or touchstone for other modern music. He must beware of such traps as that which caught a certain admirer of Stravinsky who adduced the horn melody on which the finale of *The Fire Bird* is based as proof of his hero's ability to write a beautiful tune—not knowing that the melody in question is that of a Russian folk-song, probably centuries old.

With "modern" music of this kind I am not concerned. It needs no introduction from me or anyone else. For my purpose, "modern music" is that (whether written yesterday or thirty years ago) which puzzles the ordinary intelligent but uninstructed listener and the conservative professional musician and strikes them as being deliberately and uselessly ugly. If some offensively intellectual person asks me how I know what puzzles the average listener, I shall reply that I don't live in a vacuum, that I hear the frankly expressed opinions of quite a number of such listeners, and that for the rest it is surely permissible to make reasonable suppositions sometimes. I have never heard my Aunt Kate's opinion of Mr. Frank Bridge's Piano Sonata. As far as I know, she has never heard it. But since her pet composers are Schumann and Mendelssohn and she admires nothing more modern than Grieg, I am fairly safe in assuming not merely that she would be puzzled by the Bridge work, but that she would heartily detest it.

To clear the ground (in this case, our own minds) then, we must find satisfactory answers to one or two questions. Of what does the modern idiom—or idioms, for there are a half dozen different ones—consist? What causes it? What is the necessity to which is supplied an outlet and a relief? Essentially it springs, as artistic progress always has sprung, from the impulse of the artist to say something new which could not be said, or could not be said so well, in the old idiom or from his desire to say the old things in a new way.

Just how gradually and tentatively each addition to the vocabulary is made will be seen when we come to discuss the gradual complication of what we call discord and the purely relative nature of the latter. For the present, all we need consider is the fact that this addition of new elements to the musical language and consequent dropping off of old ones, very much like the process of cell-renewal which constantly goes on in the human body, is as gradual as it is inevitable. In cases where it is not gradual—when a composer suddenly starts composing in the whole-tone scale, which has not and cannot have any roots in the past any more than a watch or a bicycle can have an ancestor, or according to some patent harmonic system of his own— our suspicions are, rightly or wrongly, aroused at once. "Can such music be genuinely alive?" we wonder. And we welcome any sign such as the touch of Massenet in *L'Après-midi* because, like the fly in the amber, it is a proof of the genuineness of the matter it is embedded in.

A young composer must at first think in terms of

the musical language of his elders, the melodic and harmonic idiom current in his environment, as surely as a baby in England must acquire the English language to speak and think in, and a baby in Germany the German language. The growing child also acquires a stock of current ideas—to which, of course, he may stick to the end of his days without materially adding to them or modifying them by the working of his own intelligence (in which case he will probably be highly respected by his fellow-citizens and is bound to be successful as a town councilor, churchwarden and Justice of the Peace). On the other hand, if he has an exceptionally active intelligence, he will be continually adding to the stock of these acquired ideas and modifying them, not only through contact with these fresh acquisitions, but by turning them over in his own mind. Creative intelligence shows itself in nothing else but this, the turning over and the fresh putting together of existing conceptions to make new ones—a process in which we see talent when it is done carefully and painstakingly, and genius when it proceeds by leaps of intuition and (to change the metaphor) the kaleidoscope appears to be shaken by some unseen hand, not apparent even to the thinker himself.

The development of the creative musician is very similar. Only in his case the stock of ideas and the

language in which to express them are almost inseparable, indeed almost identical. Not quite, however, for a
young Beethoven can take over the musical speech of
his elders and say something fresh in it, and the young
Scriabin contrived to say in Chopin's idiom things
which Chopin himself had never said, just as the middle of *L'Après-midi* is not an echo of some thought of
Massenet's but a Debussyish idea imperfectly expressed
in the language of Massenet. A mediocre composer
goes on talking in the language of the past, though he
may, of course, *ape* the language of the present in the
hope of disguising his mediocrity by speaking a tongue
which most people do not understand well enough to
criticize what is said in it. He may not actually echo
the ideas of the past, though a composer of the caliber
of Rachmaninov, for instance, finds the existing vocabulary quite sufficient for all his needs. But if new
ideas and new vocabulary are not absolutely inseparable
in music, they are so nearly one that no composer of
the first rank has been able to say all he wanted to
without remolding the current musical language into
at least a distinct dialect of his own to say it in. The
progressive composer (the Berlioz-Wagner type) actually adds new "words" to the language—new chords,
new and bold progressions. Even the non-progressive
(the Bach-Brahms type) who in no way contributes

to the difficulty of the ever-changing problem of modernism, modifies the existing vocabulary to suit the ideas he wants to express, giving entirely new values and meanings to the old "words."

It would seem needless to emphasize the inevitability of progress, of this continual enrichment of the musical language. It seems as obvious as the facts of tides and seasons. And yet I have met quite a number of people, otherwise apparently intelligent, who could not understand why the musical language of Wagner was not good enough, with perhaps a very little modification, for the modern composer—or, apparently, why Wagner was not content with Beethoven's. Our special difficulty to-day, of course, is that the language of so many modern composers seems to be not an extension of that of the last century, but a totally different one. That is partly an illusion caused by our lack of perspective. We are too close to the phenomenon to see it clearly. But it is also the consequence of some real breaks in continuity, of the fact that during the last fifty years or so the most important additions to the musical vocabulary have been made not by one outstanding master, but by a number of minor composers whose contributions have been curiously different and some of whom—for instance, Debussy, Busoni, Reger, Scriabin and Schoenberg—have been consciously interested in the theoretical possibilities of an extended or renewed vocabulary as hardly any of the older masters were. The beginning of the present century was disastrously rich in theory-ridden composers, and even those moderns who are not actually theory-ridden seem to be all too conscious of their processes. And, as usual, self-consciousness has resulted in awkwardness and exaggeration.

So, from one cause and another, an unfortunate (and probably unprecedented) situation has been reached. Composers have, in the last fifty years or so, revised and extended the musical vocabulary so drastically that the average intelligent listener has had far more than his usual difficulty in keeping pace with them. It is only natural to expect him to be bothered by innovations. It takes a little time for his ear, the normal ear of his generation, to get so accustomed to the innovation as to accept what the composer and the intelligent executant, continually living with it, have long come to consider as a commonplace of musical life. But in the past his ear always has learned to accept innovations. His difficulty in recent years has been that the innovations have come so thick and fast and from such different directions that his bewildered ear has revolted, unable to cope with the rush. Having been unable to pick up the new idioms gradually as they were introduced, he is now confronted with what is to all intents and purposes a foreign language. If the English language were seized and molded by a tiny but authoritative minority of intellectuals, scientific philologists with a passion for experiment, the man-in-the-street would in just the same way soon find the cultured classes talking and writing a language different from his own. The language of the intellectuals might easily make a leap as big as that from Chaucerian English to Shakespearian English in a generation, while that of the man-in-the-street would go on jogging along at the usual rate of progress.

Preserving the "foreign language" analogy, too useful to be rejected on account of its imperfections, we shall find that it indicates the right method of approach to modern music. How do you learn to speak and understand a foreign tongue? By two means, each useless without the other. You must learn its grammar to know *why* the native speaks as he does. And you must have any amount of practice in listening to the spoken language, to get your ear accustomed to its inflections and so on. You cannot learn a language *merely* by going among the people and listening to them—though that is what most people seem to try to do with modern music. Without the clues, the grammar and the nucleus of a vocabulary, their conversation will sound a mere meaningless jabber. Nor, on the other hand, can one learn to understand a language by poring over grammars and vocabularies alone. We all know the virtues of the good old English method of teaching languages at school, which leaves, or used to leave, the victim with an astonishing command of French irregular verbs and a complete inability to understand an excited Frenchman.

And so it is with modern music. You need some sort of guide to the composers' vocabulary and syntax, but no amount of knowledge of the why and wherefore of their musical speech will make that language your own, as natural to you as Bach's or Wagner's, without a great deal of keen listening practice. If you are not prepared to tackle the difficulty of the modern musical idiom in the same spirit that you would tackle the learning of Spanish, if you decided to take up Spanish as a hobby, you must resign yourself to the fact that modern music is not for you. Your understanding of it will be limited to the isolated phrases you can pick up casually here and there. The loss will be yours only, and no one will mind very seriously even if you consequently make yourself unintentionally funny on the correspondence page of *The Radio Times*.

But if you are genuinely keen you must realize that ultimately the one thing that matters is the "getting-used-to" process. No one can help you in that, though you need guidance as to *what* to get used to. As we shall see in the next chapter, the whole history of harmonic development is simply a record of the human ear's getting used to one degree of discord after another and accepting it as pleasant and concordant. Your task, in a nutshell, is to get your ear so accustomed to the modern idiom that a progression like this from Goossens' *Four Conceits:*—

EXAMPLE I

(*J. & W. Chester, London*)

sounds as normal as one of *Hymns A. and M.* By far the best way of "getting accustomed" is the good old-fashioned one of hammering things out for yourself at the piano. No one could learn a foreign language solely through the ear, though language is, quite as much as music, primarily an affair of sound. The student must *see* the foreign words and sentences; he has to learn to read and write them. And the parallel holds good with regard to music. The mere listener, no matter how much or how keenly he listens, necessarily remains an outsider. A little playing-and-listening is worth any amount of listening only.

Most of the best modern piano music is, admittedly, dreadfully difficult. It needs sensitive handling and a more than competent technique to make it sound in the least like what the composer heard mentally when he put the notes on paper. You are possibly incapable of even reading some of these progressions of modern chords, each with a handful of accidentals like a bunch of grapes hanging in front of it. And you would almost certainly be unable to detect your wrong notes, though (it is perhaps necessary to remind you) the right notes do really matter quite as much in Bartók as in Beethoven. We seem to have come across a very awkward obstacle, then, at the very beginning. But there *is* a certain amount of not very difficult modern piano music, not quite of the highest value but very useful for your purpose: albums of short pieces such as Goossens' *Kaleidoscope* and *Four Conceits* (Chester), Warlock's *Folk Song Preludes* (Augener), Hindemith's *Reihe kleiner Stücke* (Schott), Toch's *Tanz- und Spielstücke* (Schott), Bartók's *Ten Easy Pieces* (Rozsnyai: Budapest), Křenek's *Twelve Short Piano Pieces*, Op. 83 (Schirmer), and the *Album des Six* (Max Eschig).

The phonograph, which ought to be such a valuable

auxiliary, is as yet of no great help since comparatively little modern music of the type useful to the student has been recorded. Radio is valuable only in the same way as, and to a less extent than, ordinary concert performances. It widens your field of vision immensely and lets you hear modern music played (usually) as it ought to be played. But for a beginning it is better to study a small area intensively.

2

MODERN HARMONY: THE
RELATIVE NATURE OF DISCORD

I DON'T think I shall be very far wrong if I assume that the chief difficulty the ordinary listener comes up against in his approach to modern music is its harmonic complication. As the man-in-the-street puts it, it is "so discordant." And by that, of course, he does not mean that, like all the music written during the last two hundred years, it is full of what the harmony textbooks call discords, i.e., chords unsatisfactory in themselves but sounding perfectly normal and satisfactory, perhaps even particularly sweet to the ear, in their proper context. By "discordant" he means "ugly and offensive to the ears." How does it come about then that music which to his untrained ear is a painful cacophony can be accepted by the intensely sensitive ear of the cultured musician with genuine pleasure? Simply because he is judging it by a different concep-

tion of dissonance and with no *understanding* of it.*
The chords to which his ear is accustomed, and which
he therefore thinks of as concordant (irrespective of
harmony-book definitions) are common chords and
inversions, dominant sevenths, diminished sevenths,
added sixths and their like. They make up practically
the whole of the music which has come within his
range of experience.

The trained, but conservatively minded, musician
is in even worse case, for his technical knowledge
fastens a heavier fetter on his ability to accept anything
a little out of the ordinary. But the modern composer
and the keen student of modern developments, who
proves *ipso facto* that he has a plastic mind, have so
accustomed themselves to more and more advanced
harmonies that they have acquired quite a different
norm of consonance. Their ears are so used to a high
degree of dissonance that they accept as "satisfactory"
(or "normal" or "consonant") a great many chords
which our out-of-date harmony textbooks classify as
discords. In this respect then they are practically in the
position of the completely uninformed man-in-the-
street, much nearer than to the position of the academic
conservative.

* I shall explain later on what I mean by "understanding" dissonance.

Both the modernist and the man-in-the-street judge by realities instead of by outworn theories, but their agreement ends there. To the man-in-the-street everything that actually *sounds* discordant to him is bad, ugly, beyond the pale. But the modernist needs the flavor of real discord. Without it music is apt to sound to him as insipid as music entirely consisting of common chords would have done to Beethoven or Schumann or Mendelssohn. And to be a discord to *his* ear —an ear with a standard of consonance different from that of the majority of musical people—to make on it a demand for progress to another more restful, more consonant chord, it must be dissonant to a degree painful to the ear of the average listener. To sum up: all musicians, whether modernists or not, understand the need of a very large element of dissonance in music —a necessity of which the uninstructed man-in-the-street is quite unaware. But modernist musicians differ from their colleagues in having a different *standard* of dissonance.

And how, it may be asked incidentally, has such a "privileged"—a conservative musician might say "depraved"—class sprung up? Did it come into being naturally or does it owe its origin to pose or overintellectualism? Merely, I think, through environment and the good fortune which has placed these people in it. To take a single point by way of example: a man who has had the whole of *Tristan* as a familiar part of the musical furniture of his mind ever since he has been old enough to take any sort of intelligent interest in music is bound to have a different norm of consonance from the musician living in an English provincial town who, until the coming of radio, has had no opportunity of knowing more about *Tristan* than can be gathered from one or two concert-performances of the Prelude and "Liebestod." And there are infinitely more musicians in that position than is realized by those who live near the hubs of musical activity.

We must remember, too, that we English (and Americans as well) as a musical nation have to pay the price of our provinciality. Possessing only one opera-establishment of the first rank in the whole country (and that, until recently, beyond the financial reach of the musical masses) we cannot expect to keep up with the vanguard of musical thought as well as can the main body of "ordinary listeners" in countries where every town of any size has long had a reasonably efficient opera-house, with popular prices, and a more than reasonably efficient orchestra. To keep to the *Tristan* illustration: the German musical man-in-the-street has long had far better opportunities of getting used to *Tristan*-esque harmony as a feature of everyday musical life than have the majority of British professional musicians. Hence, perhaps, the comparative conservatism of the modern British composer.

But our business at present is to lap up as much of the spilled milk as we can, not to water it with our salt tears. We have to recognize the fact that, whatever the reason, modernist musicians (still a minority, but a very powerful and important minority) *have* naturally acquired a norm of consonance altogether different from that of the average concert-goer. (Naturally that norm varies with individuals; individual norms must cover each degree of the whole scale between that of Arnold Schoenberg and that of the village organist.)

All this talk of consonance and dissonance as purely relative things may be confusing to those who are accustomed to think of a minor common chord as a concord and a dominant seventh as a discord. But they *are* only relative terms and never have been anything else. There is no scientific ground for the drawing of an absolute line between concords and discords. Science can only tell us that a (harmony-textbook) concord is relatively less dissonant, or more consonant if you like, than a (harmony-textbook) discord. Since in practice musicians have always regarded as concords those harmonies which at that particular period in the history of music they could listen to as complete and satisfactory in themselves, not calling for resolution, it would be more rational to speak of "satisfactory" and "unsatisfactory," or "normal" and "abnormal," chords rather than of "concords" and "discords." In the Middle Ages even thirds and sixths were regarded as dissonant intervals. Then came a period during which the major third was accepted as consonant but the minor third was not. A relic of this feeling persisted till Bach's day in the "Tierce de Picardie," a major chord at the end of a piece in a minor key.

Of the twenty-four pieces in minor keys in the first book of Bach's *Forty-eight*, only one (the G sharp minor Fugue) ends on a minor chord. So we see that even when composers had grown quite accustomed to the minor triad, it still took them some time to accept it as normal enough to end a piece with. The frontier dividing consonance and dissonance has continually been altered in accordance with general feeling on the point, and our present textbook distinction records only the general feeling during the period (roughly) from Bach to Wagner, admittedly an extraordinarily important period in musical history—but only a period.

It is worth while to trace the evolution of a textbook discord from its birth to its acceptance by the modern ear as a concord. Take the case of the chord commonly known as the "added sixth." A nineteenth-century theorist would have "explained" it as a "third inversion of the dominant eleventh," an explanation which serves well enough for pigeonhole purposes but is, practically, pure nonsense. There can hardly be any doubt that this particular chord came into being in the most natural way—in other words, by accident. Take one of the most familiar of harmonic progressions:—

EXAMPLE 2

What could be more natural than that, in singing this, the upper voice moving from G to B should take the A as a passing note on its way? And behold the added sixth was created (y). But it was accepted at first only *because of its context*. That is a very important point. Sounded alone, that chord y would have jarred on all sensitive ears of the period. But musicians, being intelligent animals, though they *actually* hear only one sound or collection of sounds (chord) at a time, have the faculty of imagining it in connection with a greater or less number of past sounds—and even future ones remembered from previous hearings of a composition.

The man "with no ear" lacks this faculty; he apprehends only one sound at a time, sensuously, and is unable to link it with its predecessors and successors. But as hardly anyone is as defective as this, we forget that to appreciate even a simple melody demands a certain amount of *intelligence*, of mental ability to grasp as a whole what is only heard a bit at a time.* The point is that anyone with the most rudimentary musical intelligence was able to accept y with his ear because he understood it with his brain—whether consciously or unconsciously.

All textbook discords won their way into the respectable musical vocabulary by some such means as this. They crept in as passing notes or suspensions (i.e., notes held over from one chord into the next, in which they are dissonant). They were at first always "prepared" in some way by the composer—to soften the blow. But as time went on, people's ears got so accustomed to them that they were able to take more and more for granted, to hear y without x before it,

---

* Ability to grasp the architecture of a great musical work as a whole is nothing but a more developed form of the same faculty, though many even of those who claim to be musical do not possess it, apparently. But then everyone knows how difficult it is to get students of the semi-musical type—members of an amateur choral society, for instance—to grasp even a single long phrase as a whole. It is simply that they are not (musically) intelligent enough.

for example. Hearing y, they took x for granted. The clash of the A against the G had already become so mild that their ears no longer demanded an explanation of where the discord came from, provided the proprieties were still satisfied by the explanation of where it was going (z). (This "taking for granted" in music is roughly analogous to our acceptance of "Don't know" for "I do not know" in colloquial speech.)

The next stage in the acceptance of the discord y into the family of concords (though not yet recognized by the textbooks) is the obvious one of dispensing with the explanation of where it is going, of taking the resolution, z, for granted, too.* Actually, the clash of G against A (the dissonant element in y) is very slight, especially when blended by the C and E, which are not only consonant with each other, but together form a consonance with either the G or the A separately; so slight that modern ears find it difficult to detect it at all. In short, to modern ears the added sixth is perfectly concordant. And even if it were not sensuously pleasant in itself, the musical intelligence would make it so by mentally supplying the resolution (z). We shall again and again find the intelligence unconsciously helping the ear in this way. Which is perfectly natural since,

* No one wants the common chords of A minor and C major to fill up the rests in measures three and seven of the Prelude to *Tristan*.

as we have already seen, the faculty of musical appreciation (even in the elementary case of a simple melody) is entirely a matter of instinctive co-operation between ear and brain.*

The added sixth, of course, always was a very mild dissonance. But its history is the history of a dozen other discords more acid in flavor but now happily acclimatized. And there are one or two other factors to be considered in our acceptance of former dissonances—for instance, the "layout" and "texture" of a chord. To nineteenth-century theorists an added sixth chord was an added sixth chord—and that was all there was to be said about it. As far as they were concerned it was intrinsically the same chord in sound † no matter how its notes were spaced out or colored in-

---

* The strong domination of the mind over the ear may be observed by playing the chords:—

EXAMPLE 3

The second chord is, theoretically, a concord, but in that context it sounds (mildly) dissonant. Logically and imaginatively it is a wrench. Yet there is no *sensuous* dissonance; it is not the ear but the mind that is aroused.

† Even though they allowed it more than one theoretical origin.

strumentally, whether bunched so as to lie under a pianist's right hand or similarly bunched and played by four horns or spread over three octaves and sounded on muted strings (to say nothing of the hundreds of more subtle and complicated ways of laying it out). It is silly to sneer at the theorists, for they only reflected the general insensitiveness to these matters of their period.

But for the last forty years at least, this "simple primrose" attitude toward chords has been definitely abandoned. We have belatedly recognized that there is no such thing as a chord-in-the-abstract. We have descended to realities and opened our ears to the fact that the layout of the notes of a chord is far more than a matter of mere balance of parts. If anyone is still in doubt on this point and as to the way it affects the question of dissonance, let him play these chords, different distributions of what harmony books would consider the *same* chord, on the piano:—

EXAMPLE 4

No one, I think, will dispute that *b* is definitely more dissonant than *a*, or that the difference would be intensified by playing *b* very loudly and *a* softly.

It is obvious, too, that the degree of dissonance of both chords would be modified by the context in which they might occur or by playing them on instruments of a different tone-color. And here we catch a first glimpse of another resource of which many modern composers take full advantage. A chord may be so laid out for various instruments that, flouting the old ideals of blend and balance, particular notes are emphasized —or so subdued that they seem only to flavor the chord rather than to form part of its substance. The ineffec- tiveness of piano reductions of modern orchestral works is due partly to this, partly to various other causes—to increasing complexity of texture and richness of color; to the fact that modern melodies are often conceived in terms of a particular instrument and lose their sensi- tiveness when transferred to the piano; but most of all to the necessity of completely altering the layout of chords to make them lie under the pianist's hands, and the impossibility of reproducing the subtleties of blended tone-color. The clash of two melodies in mod- ern counterpoint can easily be made more acceptable to the ear by careful scoring, while on the piano the effect may be absolutely intolerable.*

* Any admirer of Delius who, delighted by one of his later and most sensitive orchestral works, experiments with it at the piano, quickly learns to his disappointment how completely the beauty of modern music may be destroyed by even a skilfully made tran-

So we have discovered not only that dissonance (like poverty) is a purely relative matter in itself, but that even the degree of apparent dissonance in any particular case may be considerably modified by various factors— the sophistication of the listener's ear, context (both general and immediate contexts: the norm of dissonance in the composition as a whole, and the nature of the actual passage in which the discord occurs), layout, instrumental color, and so on. And I am not sure that, after all, the most important factor is not immediate context, for the ear will accept almost anything that it can *understand*. The isolated chord:—

EXAMPLE 5

is intolerable even to an ear accustomed to hearing a great deal of modern music, but we can accept this sound almost without turning a hair when we hear it in this context in Holst's *Hymn of Jesus:*—

scription. There are exceptions, of course. But as a rule the only modern music really effective on the piano is that which has been written for the instrument in the first place. Modern piano arrangements are generally useful only after you have heard the work two or three times in its proper medium and can bring your memory and imagination to your aid.

EXAMPLE 6

(Stainer & Bell, London)

where it obviously results from the perfectly clear movement of one set of parts (the second chorus) and the stationariness of the others (the first chorus). And Gian-Carlo Menotti in the last scene of *The Consul* can go even further than Holst, thanks to his low dynamic marking, his scoring and (not least) his dramatic pretext:

EXAMPLE 7

(Schirmer, New York)

But when a composer feels that a chord is not dissonant enough to need resolution he naturally announces the fact to a more or less interested world by *not* resolving it, by treating it as the concord it has actually become so far as his ear is concerned. (That is, unless his education has been too much for him and he feels he must give an orthodox resolution purely from a sense of duty, or from habit, or so as not to shock his poor old parents.) So Verdi in 1892, at the end of a blameless career as a thoroughly conservative harmonist, realizing as Chopin had done long before that (in spite of what the textbooks said they were) second inversions of dominant sevenths gave him no sensation of discordance, calmly wrote a row of them near the end of the first scene of Act III of *Falstaff* without bothering to resolve even the last one (except by implication three bars later):—

EXAMPLE 8

(*Ricordi, Milan*)

just as if they had been simple common chords. They had, in fact, become only richer concords. "Nothing very daring in that passage," you say. Exactly. And from 1892 it was only a step (just another major third, to be precise) to 1918:—

EXAMPLE 9

(*J. & W. Chester, London*)

which is the opening of the last of Goossens' *Kaleido-scope* pieces. The only difference is that whereas Verdi is content with second inversions of sevenths, Goossens likes the slightly more piquant flavor of second inversions of major ninths. (Never mind the names of the chords if you don't understand them; listen to the sounds.)

The process of "getting used to" a more acute norm of dissonance, then, is not quite the same thing (as some of our conservative friends seem to think) as ruining the sensitiveness of one's ear. Actually, just the reverse happens; the ear is trained to greater alertness by the necessity of analyzing more complicated sounds. The modern ear, it is true, has had to learn tolerance of certain things, just as sensitive ears had to do when "equal temperament" tuning was introduced and later when valve instruments took the place of "natural" brass in the orchestra. Palestrina would have found the tuning of Bach's clavichord excruciating until he had got used to it. Mozart probably turned in his grave for years when people first took to playing all his horn-parts on valve-horns in F. Acceptance of these things does debase the ear; equal temperament *is* bad in comparison with the pure scale—and yet Bach, who (presumably) was not tone-deaf, made practical propaganda for it. In tolerating not quite satisfactory compromise in little things for the sake of progress in much bigger ones we are only acting in the same spirit as Bach.

3

MODERN HARMONY:
NEW CHORDS AND THE
NEW ATTITUDE TO CHORDS

SIDE by side with the gradual acceptance of familiar discords as concords another process has gone on in modern music—the invention of entirely new chords. Obviously this is quite a different matter from the gradual acclimatization of exotic, but "recognized," discords. As different as the coining of a new word is from the adoption of a familiar and convenient foreign word. That is a natural, this (generally) an artificial process. It is not always artificial, for a composer like Holst or Delius will sometimes use a chord "that never was" simply because he likes it or because he wants its particular flavor to express something. Or it may be produced in passing by the movement of his parts. Ex. 6 is an instance of the latter. And here is an example of the former, from the end of Delius's *Sea Drift:*—

EXAMPLE 10

(*Universal Edition, Vienna*)

where the chord *x* is both piercingly beautiful (in this context) and poignantly expressive. Even that *might* be explained theoretically, as nearly all Delius's apparently haphazard chords can be (and more easily than this one). But only a pedant would demand an explanation; we may be sure that the composer used the chord empirically, without wasting a moment's thought on its possible etymology.

Single new chords of this kind which have come into being naturally and fulfill a definite purpose, can worry nobody. But a very real problem is presented by the artificial chords and harmonic systems deliberately invented by certain modern composers. Here, in effect, are poets not content to take every imaginable liberty with the old vocabulary and the old syntax; they must have an entirely new language, or at least a new vocabu-

lary—an artificial musical Esperanto of their own de-
vising. On the face of it, it looks like a pose. Musical
ideas and the language in which they are expressed
being so nearly identical, it seems that spontaneous
musical ideas can hardly be expressed in an artificial
language, that this Esperanto can only express ideas
as purely brain-spun as itself.

That is true, so far as it goes, but against it we have
to remember that harmony is nowadays more than
ever a "color," something added to the original conception and not *necessarily* an integral part of it. And we
must bear in mind, too, the fact that a very little
familiarity with a new harmonic system is sufficient to
set a man's fancy playing with it, just as it normally
plays with the everyday elements of diatonic scales
and arpeggios of familiar chords in the invention of
melodies. A composer who has devised a "language"
will learn to think naturally in it soon enough. The
point is, of course: Was the new language indispensable
for the saying of these things? Could they not have
been said in the old familiar tongue? Only the fact that
the new speech can express ideas that the old could
not have expressed at all—or, at any rate, not nearly
so well—really justifies such a radical change of idiom.
Musical Esperantists like Scriabin and Schoenberg always rest under a suspicion, just or unjust, that they

are either merely theorizing for their own amusement or trying to give their ideas a factitious novelty.

But we must not be too hasty with our condemnation. It may be useful to trace the steps by which Scriabin, to take an outstanding example of a musical Esperantist, arrived at this branching-out point. The fact that Scriabin is now thought very little of need not concern us; it would take us too far out of our way to debate whether he was over-rated thirty or forty years ago or whether he is under-rated now. Scriabin, as is well known, began his career as an innocent and single-minded worshiper—and, it is not unfair to say, deliberate imitator—of Chopin. Later, shadows of Liszt, Schumann and Wagner fall across his music. In short, he was perfectly content, as every composer is at first content, not merely to use the language of his predecessors but to repeat under various disguises the essence of their thoughts. And, as always happens if the younger man really has the root of the matter in him, Scriabin's own personality soon began to show through and, as it developed, to find the harmonic idiom of Chopin and Liszt less and less adequate for the expression of what he wanted to say. The well-known set of *Twenty-Four Preludes*, Op. 11, written in his early twenties, shows Scriabin at that point in his development where his own musical individuality, his own way of thinking, was just beginning to break out of the Chopinesque chrysalis, but at the same time still found the Chopinesque harmonic idiom rich enough and supple enough to convey his thought. Op. 11, No. 15, for instance, is pure Scriabin in essence but firmly anchored in the past so far as its harmonic substance is concerned.

The very gradual complication of Scriabin's harmony by the ever bolder use of what the theorist calls appoggiaturas, passing-notes, and so on can easily be traced up to, say, the orchestral *Poem of Ecstasy*, Op. 54, and the Fifth Piano Sonata, Op. 53 (written a dozen or so years later than the Op. 11 Preludes). "Foreign" notes are introduced frankly as passing strangers into more usual chords and progressions and then, when the composer himself has got used to them, are allowed to stay on as friends and members of the family. Intensive study at the piano of a few pieces from Scriabin's transition period *taken in chronological order* is invaluable as an initiation not only into Scriabin's personal harmonic system but into modern harmony in general.*

* The *Scriabin Album* of thirty-three pieces which the late Dr. Eaglefield Hull edited for Boosey and Hawkes is useful for this purpose, though the vitally important link-period between Op. 16 and Op. 37 is insufficiently covered. Hull's selection lays a little too much stress on Scriabin's points of departure and arrival and not quite enough on the way of his journeying. And his "suggested titles" are unfortunate. Nevertheless the *Album* offers a helpful approach to Scriabin.

The *Poem of Ecstasy* and the Fifth Sonata may be considered as the high-water marks of Scriabin's gradual, easily traceable, development. By a perfectly natural path he had traveled harmonically all the way from Chopin to a point where his ear could accept without alarm an advanced degree of discord and where he found it absolutely necessary to employ subtle and complicated chords to express the elusive "soul-states" and spiritual aspirations in which he had become more and more deeply interested. He had from the beginning shown a fondness for the flavor of chords built up of fourths; it peeps out, for instance, in the forty-fifth bar of the innocent-looking *Impromptu à la mazur* in C major, Op. 2, No. 3, written while the composer was still a student at the Moscow Cadet School:—

EXAMPLE II

So the ground was in every way prepared for the Esperanto in which *Prometheus* and the last five piano sonatas are written. If Scriabin's later harmonic system is an artificial language, he at any rate arrived at it naturally enough. The basic idea—that a chord built up in fourths with notes selected from the natural harmonic series might be accepted as a "normal" chord (or concord, as we should say)—only served to crystallize what the composer had already had in his mind in a fluid state. The fearsome "mystic chord" of *Prometheus* itself:—

EXAMPLE 12

may be artificial and the music spun from it false and artificial, but it is easy to understand how Scriabin, with that fondness for the harmonic flavor of fourths and with an ear grown accustomed to subtle and acute dissonance, could accept it as "normal" and think as naturally in terms of it as Mozart thought in terms of ordinary major and minor triads.

But a composer who advances so far in a direction conditioned almost entirely by his personal and peculiar tastes and interests and by a personal assumption (such as Scriabin's assumption that the natural harmonic series is consonant for practical purposes)—such a composer is asking rather a lot when he expects the musical world in general to accompany him. Only a little band of disciples will take the trouble to learn his private language, and so finally he is left preaching in the wilderness, his disciples die or drift away—and the next generation does not understand what he talked about. They turn up his sermons and find them written in a sort of cipher-jargon to which they have no clue. (And the little they can make out seems to deal with matters in which they are probably not in the least interested.) This is what has happened to Scriabin. His harmonic advance was a solitary exploration down a side-track. The rest of the musical world has kept to the high road or, at least, wandered well within sight of it, contributing to the mass advance.

This, of course, is the kernel of the matter: that all language and all modification of it (including the musical equivalent) is produced by the mass of cultivated people and occasionally the uncultivated,* not by individuals or even by groups. *They* may only make their small contribution, and if they refuse to speak a dialect having a great deal in common with the language of the majority they must expect to be gaped at by the barbarians in the crowd and ignored, after a little interested study, by its intelligent members.

Chords built up of fourths, instead of thirds like all the recognized textbook chords, have fascinated quite

* Folk-music, for instance, and (to a slight extent) jazz.

a number of modern harmonic experimenters, however. Schoenberg has theorized about them at considerable length, though on lines quite different from Scriabin's. But the best approach to such chords will be found in Holst's music—for instance, the opening chorus of the finale of his *Choral Symphony:*

EXAMPLE 13

(Novello, London)

where the logic of this sort of chord-building is laid as bare as it can be. It is easy to see the possibilities (and limitations) of endless switch-backing offered by these pilings up of two or three perfect fourths. Naturally an infinitely wider range is opened up by the use of other than perfect fourths.

Still, the perfect fourth and fifth are symptomatic; with the modern composer they take the place occupied by the third and sixth in the older music, by a natural process of reaction from the over-familiar. (And we should remember, incidentally, that the third and sixth themselves actually came as a reaction against the medieval tyranny of the fourth and fifth.) Nor is this necessarily a sign that composers are merely seeking newness for the sake of newness. It is clear that Holst, for example, always (that is, since his rather sickly early compositions, now completely forgotten) has liked the pure, astringent flavor of these intervals. Everyone who has heard his *Ode to Death* must remember the cold, serene beauty of the bare open fifths at the beginning and end of that work, and some of the figuration in *Jupiter* (*The Planets*) immediately prepares the ear for chords like those in Ex. 13. People who talk loosely about "modern harmony" as if it were all tarred, or whitewashed, with the same brush would do well to consider the fact (hardly questionable, I think) that these dry, alkaline chords, like the acidities of the later Schoenberg (*Pierrot Lunaire*, for instance) are symptoms of violent reaction from the romanticism which produced such over-ripe, if delightful, fruit as Ex. 10.

One other sort of modern chord frequently heard must be mentioned here, belonging neither to the purely empirical class nor to any definite system of harmony. Liberal-minded theorists, however, recognize these

chords as a definite type and (for convenience' sake
have) christened them "added-note" chords. As the
name implies, they consist of the notes of an ordinary
chord *plus* an added note by way of seasoning. The
modern composer finds an unseasoned common chord
altogether too insipid. So Stravinsky, for instance, in
the finale of *The Fire Bird*, harmonizes the final variation in this way:—

EXAMPLE 14

where an older composer would have written:—

EXAMPLE 15

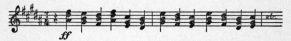

Stravinsky's harmonization, at once richer and more
pungent, might be regarded as a decoration of Ex. 15
by added notes. A year or two after *The Fire Bird*, in
Le Sacre du Printemps, Stravinsky devised a more
daring and peculiarly ambiguous form of added-note
chord: a triad with both major and minor third simultaneously. That, too, has in the course of forty years
passed into the normal contemporary harmonic idiom,

and in the first movement of his Violin Concerto of 1947 William Schuman freely uses not only such major-minor triads but higher-power chords built on the same principle:

EXAMPLE 16

(*Schirmer, New York*)

A passage, too long for quotation, in the Sarabande of Debussy's *Pour le Piano* provides an interesting illustration of the way added-note chords first found their way into the vocabulary. It is that which begins with measure 35 (*trés soutenu*), where the reiterated C sharps act as the thin end of the wedge. Like the D sharps in the next bar but one, they can be accepted as a brief "inside pedal" effect. And once *they* are accepted, the way is smoothed for the acceptance of what follows. It is worth noting that although all the chords in the descending eighth-note passages are familiar discords, recognized and labeled by the harmony books, the ear does not hear them as such but as a series of six-four chords (second inversions of common chords) *with added notes*. And, of course, to the modern ear the whole passage of seven measures is consonant, though according to textbook teaching it is entirely dissonant.*

This Debussy passage, like that from *The Fire Bird*, illustrates yet another modern tendency—the "side-slipping" of chords. Harmony preceding the classical period was more or less the result of the separate movement of independent parts (as may be seen from its reduction to its lowest terms in the ordinary four-part hymn) and the touchstone of good harmony was, normally, the sense of progressive movement it gave. But the modern musician has tended more and more to keep to a chord for a while, if he likes its flavor, simply moving it sideways *en bloc* as we have already seen Verdi and Goossens doing in Exs. 8 and 9 and as William Schuman does in measures 2–3 of Ex. 16. The contrapuntal ancestry of harmony, obvious enough in

* The whole of this Sarabande, which is technically much less difficult than the majority of Debussy's piano compositions, amply repays study. Note at measures 23–28, and again six measures before the end of the piece, the perfectly natural use of chords built up of perfect fourths.

-< 57 >-

Bach, was already pretty thoroughly concealed by the time of Haydn and Beethoven, and in these examples by Verdi, Goossens, Stravinsky, Debussy and Schuman it has disappeared altogether. And whereas in the Verdi, Goossens and Schuman examples the chords are still definitely "harmony" in the old sense of "background accompaniment to the melody," they are doubtfully even that in the other two cases. The harmony here seems to have become a mere thickening out of the melody itself, so to speak.

In other words, the true melody in these passages is a continuous *block* of sound, instead of the customary thin one-note line of sound. Sometimes such chords are rigidly side-slipped, without the least modification; sometimes, as in these particular instances from the Debussy Sarabande and *The Fire Bird*, they are slightly modified, but the principle remains the same.* Thus an evolutionary cycle has completed itself. The single part multiplied gave us polyphony. Polyphony, gradually crystallizing, produced the homophony of Beethoven and Schumann and has finally solidified into a single "thick" part—though that, of course, is only one of a number of simultaneous developments.

But evolution brings matters back, not to their

* The difference is roughly analogous to that between a "real" and a "tonal" answer in a fugue.

starting-point, but to another point in the spiral immediately above it. The single part has come back, but as a chord-line instead of a line of single notes. And evolution continues. The next step is a counterpoint of these thickened out melodies, and it has already been taken by practically every contemporary composer. This is how Vaughan Williams takes it in the first movement of his *Pastoral Symphony*:—

EXAMPLE 17

(*Curwen, London*)

a passage which should be listened to simply as a piece of two-part writing. The fact that each "part" is in a different key is more alarming on paper than in actual performance. Here again the intellect helps the ear, for the mind can easily follow the two strands separately from the point where the key "splits"; and when they are reunited a few bars later it is only as if a normal, long-held dissonance had been resolved. The shock to the ear in this really daring passage is reduced to a minimum by two circumstances: (1) Each "part" taken separately is quite consonant even in the old sense; (2) The highest, and therefore most noticeable, voices in each "part"—the "top edges," so to speak, of the blocks—also go comfortably side by side. The filling out of these simple diatonic melodies into chord-blocks has the effect of adding a second dimension to the music, while the contrasting of two simultaneous keys adds a third. A few hearings of the passage will soon remove any doubts of its exquisite beauty. And the ear which can accept this is well on the way to understanding, though not necessarily admiration, of the most daring experiments in polytonality.

4

POLYTONALITY, ATONALITY, AND THE QUARTER-TONE SYSTEM

"POLYTONALITY" is a horrid word, and it describes what is to a great many people a still more horrid practice, the writing of music in several keys simultaneously. True, the threat of "poly" has not often been fulfilled. Milhaud has written passages in five or even six keys at once (e.g., in the third of his *Cinq Symphonies pour Petit Orchestre*) and the hero of *The Constant Nymph* wrote a *Symphony in Three Keys*. But generally "poly" implies nothing worse than "two," which is just as well, for few of us can manage to listen to more than two keys simultaneously without intolerable discomfort.

As the example from Vaughan Williams shows, polytonality can be used to produce new subtle effects of beauty in passing, but it still remains to be proved whether it is capable of extended use *effectively*. A great deal of professedly polytonal music looks more audacious than it sounds (e.g., Goossens' *Dance Memories*, from the *Four Conceits*). One finds on examination that the composers have not dared to be as naughty as they pretend; they write C sharps in the treble and D flats in the bass, and hope we shall think the clash very daring. There is a typical example of this leaning of two simultaneous keys against a common prop in the form of a note common to both in sound, though "spelled" differently in each (A flat = G sharp), in Aaron Copland's Piano Concerto: *

EXAMPLE 18

(*Cos Cob Press*)

where the mere aggregations of notes, if taken out of their context and undistinguished by the opposed sonorities of piano and orchestra, would sound just like

---

* No one can be more naïve than a really sophisticated modern composer. More than one of these very up-to-date people would, I am sure, spell the common chord of C major "D double flat, F flat, G, B sharp," but for the fear of provoking a strike of music-engravers. A well-known English composer has interpolated a meas-

added-note chords. Again, as in Ex. 17, the opposed chord-blocks—taken separately—are very simple.

The modern composer likes lines which stand out from each other, instead of blending and so to a certain extent losing their identity. His orchestration emphasizes that. The rich, sonorous muddle (as it often was) beloved of the generation of Wagner-worshipers is gone, if not for ever at least for a decade or two. Modern scoring is hard, transparent and clear-cut. To the same end the modern composer will often throw a melody into higher relief by setting it against a background of "foreign" harmony. And polytonality obviously offers a first-rate means of making parts stand out from each other; the music proceeds simultaneously on two different planes, as in Exs. 17 and 18. It is futile to object, as a good many do, that this sort of writing reduces counterpoint to a farce, that "if all sorts of clashes are permitted" anyone can write fugues. No artist of any importance is simple enough to think that because all things are lawful all things are likewise expedient. Part-weaving, to be of any value, must be guided by a genuine creative impulse as certainly nowadays when "all sorts of clashes are permitted" as in

ure of 13/16 time in a 3/4 passage in his Piano Sonata, for the sake of an odd sixteenth-note which anyone else would have incorporated in a quintuplet group.

the days of Bach. The other sort of counterpoint, that into which the breath of life has never been breathed, is no better if all the "rules" are kept than if they are all flouted. The trouble with modern music is simply that the idiom is so strange to most people that they are quite unable to distinguish between dead matter and living flesh. (And not everyone can do that even in the case of Bach, judging by the hopelessly uncritical attitude toward him of the average musician to-day.)

Polytonal music is naturally intolerable to those who apprehend music sensuously and with a minimum use of the intelligence. Their ears hear the clashes but not the why-and-wherefore of them which is all that makes them bearable. Where modern music of this type is concerned, *tout comprendre* is to forgive at any rate quite a lot. Distinguishing and clearly following the unfolding of the separate strands of polytonal counterpoint, the expert ear (even though it may dislike the sounds they produce in combination) is at least listening to what the composer intended it to hear, in other words, listening on the same lines as the composer himself. But the sort of person who imagines he is enjoying the woven tapestry of a Bach organ fugue, when he is really only reveling sensuously in the gorgeous, barbaric confusion of sound which the average provincial English organist foists on him as Bach, never will be able to make head or tail of "this modern stuff." He can't even hear it (in the true sense). He may be able to wallow at times in the more sentimental Delius or get mildly intoxicated with the more obvious and "tuney" parts of *Petrushka*, but as soon as a little concentration and musical intelligence are called for he is lost. To such a merely sensuous listener Bach's counterpoint is at any rate a jolly hullabaloo, but polytonal counterpoint *et hoc genus omne* must sound like the souls of politicians wailing in Hades.

The only real difficulty that confronts the keen, intelligent listener is presented by the unusual, and often apparently irrational, behavior of the individual melodic lines—which naturally sets his instinct at fault. Just as a cacophonous chord is more acceptable if the listener understands its relative position in the scheme of things, it is all the more unpleasant if it seems to have been brought about deliberately yet purposelessly, by the eccentric twists in one of the melodic lines. But this is a specifically melodic difficulty and we must leave the discussion of modern melody till later.

Theoretically at the other extreme from polytonality, but in practice meeting it in the No-Man's-Land of dissonance, is atonality, the doing away with all keys and key-centers. As far as one can see, this delightfully anarchistic practice had two parents (like so many of us), the excessive chromaticism of the later *Tristan*-worshipers and the whole-tone scale. The whole-tone scale was an admittedly artificial device invented by the Russian pioneers of seventy years ago, Glinka and Dargomizhsky, and used by them and their successors (Borodin, for instance) for special effects, very limited purposes of expression. Except Dargomizhsky, in the statue music of his Don Juan opera, *The Stone Guest*, they wrote only the actual scale itself, not music composed in the whole-tone mode. Later composers, such as Debussy, have not been so moderate. No. 2 of Debussy's first book of *Préludes* (*Voiles*) is almost entirely written in the whole-tone mode, and the pianist whose limited technique puts Debussy out of his reach will find a simple example in No. 9 of Bartók's *Ten Easy Pieces*. All sorts of objections have been made to the whole-tone scale: it is artificial—no composer thinks spontaneously in terms of whole-tones only; it is limited to two "keys" only (the series C, D, E, F sharp, etc., and the series D flat, E flat, F, G, etc.)—and never the twain can meet, for they have not a single note in common, though many composers dodge from one to the other (as Bartók does in the piece mentioned). But the most notable weakness of the whole-tone scale is its want of a key-note, a note that can be felt as "home."

All the steps being equal, no degree of the scale has any special function or peculiar relationship to any of the others. All natural scales, from our everyday major and minor scales and the now revived medieval modes to the most exotic oriental scales, have what the Irishman called "a regular irregularity" of intermingled tones and semitones which establishes definite landmarks in the tonal landscape. The whole-tone scale, on the other hand, is a perfectly flat and featureless desert. There is nothing in it from which we can get our bearings. All its degrees having equal value, none has any special qualification as a nucleus or tonic. The most a composer can do to give whole-tone music a center of gravity is to create a sort of artificial tonic by centering his music on a certain note. But as a tonic loses most of its value when tonality is destroyed, there is not much advantage in that.

Excessive chromaticism has led ultimately to the same result. A single scale of twelve notes is admittedly more flexible than two scales of six notes, but it suffers from most of the same disadvantages. One wilderness of semitones is hardly more habitable than a couple of deserts of whole-tones. And it was probably consciousness of this which at one time drove one or two of the more daring explorers in these wastes of chromaticism (the Czech, Alois Hába, for instance) to experiment with intervals smaller than the semitone. If excessive chromaticism resulted in absolute liberty, perfect equality and appalling monotony, quarter-tones had to be called in to break up the paralyzing evenness of the semitones.

One admires the courage of these experimenters who found the wilderness uninhabitable but still pressed on, refusing to turn back to diatonic safety and comfort. But unfortunately their quarter-tone music, like Indian music (which always has employed microtones), merely sounds to most of us like normal chromatic music played out of tune. Apart altogether from its artificiality and its impracticability on any but stringed instruments (or specially constructed keyed instruments), quarter-tone music demands a keenness of perception which is beyond even the average cultivated ear at present. One can only say that it may be the music of the future.

But polytonality and atonality are definitely playing an important part in the music of the present. For the most part composers are content to use them, as Vaughan Williams does in the *Pastoral* passage, episodically—as an extension of the normal means of expression. They mix their keys or abandon recognizable tonality altogether for a time, but they are usually careful not to stay in the wood too long. Keys are no longer "established" as in the old days. Rows of chords and stretches of passage-work entirely foreign to a key are introduced without the least suggestion of modulation, but rather as a sort of spice to (or extension on another plane of) the key, so that a passage may be "E flattish" rather than definitely "in E flat." But tonality remains all the same in most cases. The modern composer's neglect to hammer home the chief key of a movement by two or three dozen *fortissimo* repetitions of the tonic chord is simply a moderate tribute to the superior musical intelligence of present-day audiences. Nevertheless, William Walton's *Portsmouth Point*, for instance, is as definitely in C major as the first movement of Beethoven's First Symphony is; though as it happens it does not contain a single common chord of C major, unadorned by added notes, from beginning to end.

The whole-hogging atonalists are, admittedly, harder nuts to crack. And those who have failed console themselves with the reflection that most people, including many whose tastes are by no means conservative, are very doubtful whether they are worth cracking. Yet this attitude to "difficult" modern art is fundamentally wrong. It is fairer to assume that the prisoner is innocent of depositing rubbish until he has been proved guilty—though, in spite of the manifest injustice of denying the value of something we admittedly do not understand, we seldom hesitate to do it. Still, in the case of Schoenberg himself there is a certain amount of definite evidence that his music is first and last *intellectual*, the very sort of thing everyone agrees is *not* genuine music when it is written in the idiom we can understand. The suspicion that it is essentially "paper" music is strengthened by the extraordinary list of corrections and improvements to the famous *Five Orchestral Pieces* which Schoenberg found it necessary to issue in 1922.

But it is very unwise to begin the study of atonal music with Schoenberg. Apart from the fact that his *Three Piano Pieces*, Op. 11, are technically too difficult for the average amateur to study very profitably at the keyboard, they propound too many hard sayings. And the six pieces of his Op. 19 are no more helpful in this respect. A far better approach, more attractive and technically easier, will be found in Ernst Toch's *Tanz- und Spielstücke*. Take the rather charming *Tanz für Ruth*, for instance—and if you fail to find it rather charming at first, persevere with it. It is definitely atonal, but slightly "A majorish," a feeling suggested by the melody of the two opening bars and by the conclusion. It is certainly not "in A," but the suspicion of A major is just enough to give the piece a tonal center of gravity.* It is all very slight, of course; a little Griegish perhaps, but full of naïve grace and sweetness, a concrete proof that advanced modernism is not incompatible with charm. It is admittedly a long way from this to Schoenberg's *Three Pieces*, yet no further than from a Grieg *Lyric Piece* to a Brahms Rhapsody. Many who have been frightened away from atonal music by its Brahmses might find a way into it through its Griegs.

* No. 8 of the same set, for all its curious combination of whole-tone scale and chromatic scale, still takes its bearings from C—a shadow tonic.

5

MODERN MELODY

IF modern harmony is a sort of obstacle to be pene-
trated, modern melody is something positive to be
grasped. The cynic, of course, says there is no such
thing. But we need not worry about him. He *will* have
his little joke. Melody matters just as much to Hindemith as it did to Haydn; it is only that his melody is of
a different nature. But then, like harmony and the
English weather, it always has been different. A contemporary of Bach's, making use of the Time-Machine,
would no doubt have considered the melodies of Haydn
and Mozart, with their comparatively short, clear-cut
rhythmic periods, deplorably undignified and suitable
only for light dance movements. A later generation,
accustomed to tunes of this kind—and no other kind
—found it difficult to recognize even Wagner's more

obvious melodies as such and was completely bothered by his "endless melody."

Fétis, who after all was not a fool (on the contrary, one of the most intelligent musicians of his day) is pilloried by Hadow * for saying of the *Tannhäuser* Overture that "beyond a poor, ill-harmonized chorale-tune . . . there is not a single spark of melody in the whole production." "To have passed over Tannhäuser's song is fatal," says Hadow. "There it stands in the middle of the *allegro*, a complete 32-measure tune, in as clear, perfect, and unmistakable a stanza as 'La ci darem' or 'God Save the Queen.' There may be differences of opinion as to its merits. . . . But to deny its existence altogether is simply to put oneself out of court on a matter of fact, and we can only infer that M. Fétis was inattentive or preoccupied." But Calvocoressi, commenting on both writers in his *Musical Criticism*, points out that "when speaking of melody Fétis, if he meant anything at all, gave the word a meaning very different from that which Hadow gives it in this crushing confutation: he probably used it as a synonym for certain particular lilts and commonplaces without which, in his mind, no 'tune' could exist."

That is our trouble to-day. We all have a habit of making unconscious definitions (controlled of course

* *Studies in Modern Music*, First Series.

by our personal limitations) and then excommunicating everything that is excluded by our definition. When the man-in-the-street talks about a "tune," he definitely means what Fétis did—something with "particular lilts and commonplaces" and an almost clockworklike rhythmical regularity. And the intelligent music-lover, though his definition may be a good deal less narrow than this, has each his own unconscious definition of melody. Naturally in forming it he is guided by example, just as a man gets his conception of a pig from the pigs he sees, without consciously deciding what distinguishes the genus "pig" from other and more pleasing inhabitants of the animal world. And as the majority of the melodies he hears, from folk-songs to Brahms *Lieder*, consist of a number of separate, more or less symmetrical phrases, neatly balancing each other, easily grasped separately and therefore not difficult to grasp as a collective whole, he is apt to conclude (naturally but wrongly) that this characteristic of being built up from clearly defined and balanced phrases is an essential feature of a melody. A better-instructed musician will go further and recognize that any voice of a Bach fugue is melodic and that Wagner's "endless melody" in his mature works is justly so called. (But even then he may recognize that it *is* a melody without being able to grasp its full beauty; ability to do that is dependent on that faculty of thinking-backward-and-forward already referred to, the faculty of mental perspective.)

But the listener must forget *all* preconceptions of what melody ought to be. It may dodge about over the widest intervals.* It may remain in one key throughout or modulate through half a dozen keys or be in no key at all. It can be as square-cut as the composer likes, or absolutely free from any metrical limitations at all—purely rhapsodic. It can be anything and do anything as long as it is (if I may adapt Clive Bell's famous definition) *significant line* in sound. It is not enough to define melody as "line," pure and simple. It must have significance. Not, of course, "meaning" in the no-nonsense-about-art-for-art's-sake sense, but aesthetic significance.

EXAMPLE 19

are lines but they obviously have little or no significance. They are mere conventional patterns and so we

* See Beethoven's Sonata in E flat, Op. 7 (measure 51 of the first movement) for a perfectly natural leap of a thirteenth in a melody.

cannot consider them melodies. But (*b*) has slightly more significance than (*a*) and so it is of the two the less far from being a melody. Bar them, i.e., give them rhythmical significance, and both would be brought a stage nearer to the condition of melody. This is the only true criterion by which we can judge a melody, not by reference to any example or any preconceived ideas as to what melody ought to be, but simply by asking: Is it significant line? What is the value of its significance?

And there, heaven knows, we still have ample grounds for quarrel. It is still open to you to claim that the significance of Schoenberg's:—

EXAMPLE 20

(*Universal Edition, Vienna*)

is about .001, that his tune is practically valueless. But you must admit, I think, that his line has some significance, in other words that it *is* a melody, whatever its quality. (For "significance," in the sense in which I am using it, is not even peculiar to the spontaneous, living product of the musico-creative faculty. It *should* be limited to that, but the presence or absence of spontaneity so often defies demonstration.) If we want some means of judging the *value* of modern melody, we shall have to try again. But we cannot fairly venture on valuation until we grasp Schoenberg's melodies as easily as we do Brahms's. Then, and then only, we shall really be in a position to know what we like and dislike. (It is reserved for half-wits to dislike what they don't understand.) In the meantime all we can do is to get rid of prejudices, of false and merely pedantic standards of judgment.

Actually, melody has changed less than any other element of music in recent years. By its nature it is more spontaneous than harmony. And what comes from the depths of a composer's unconsciousness, instead of from his intellect, naturally draws on the materials stored in those depths—memories of the music of the past. The purely melodic element in the music of a great many modern composers is predominantly diatonic, and not infrequently obvious to the point of banality. The modern Anglo-Saxon composer is particularly fond of dressing up harmless diatonic tunes in the most daring chromatic clothes. Such a modish garb does not always suit the quiet, old-fashioned type of girl; especially if she happens to be a folk-tune, as she very often is. It takes a Delius to get away with a *Brigg Fair*. Too often the tune is altogether overdressed. Though better that, perhaps, than such an exposure of a tune's distressing nakedness as Honegger makes in his *Pastorale d'été*. And what are we to make of Paul Creston's harmonizations of plainsong in his Third Symphony, *Three Mysteries*?

EXAMPLE 21

(Schirmer, New York)

He could plead, of course, that his harmony is no more foreign to the melody than some of Bach's chromatic harmonizations of certain perfectly diatonic chorale tunes. But it takes a Bach to get away with the latter part of "Was mein Gott will" in the *Matthew Passion*.

But though matings of the new harmony with the old melody too often seem a little unnatural, they are most useful to the listener trying to accustom his palate to the modern idiom. To change the metaphor, a diatonic melody provides him with a sort of handrail through the fog of dissonant harmony. But diatonic melody can hardly be considered modern, in the "difficult" sense, even when it escapes from the "particular lilts and commonplaces," the rhythmical regularity and the symmetrical phrases, into the open field of more or less rhapsodical "endless melody." For "endless melody" is nothing new to those who know their Bach and their Wagner. Its rhapsodizing is no freer now than it ever was. It is, as it always has been, melodic prose as contrasted with the verse of the symmetrical, patterned "tune"—and that is all there is to be said about it. It has always been less easy to appreciate, because it demands a more developed sense of musical perspective before it can be grasped as a whole. And that difficulty is naturally increased when the melodic line takes other than diatonic or nearly-diatonic forms. But the *new* difficulty lies in these other forms, not in the unsymmetrical build of the melody. (And, of course, both the prose and verse types of melody exist side by side in the new music as in the old.)

What makes modern melody sound "unmelodious" to the musical man-in-the-street is neither its occasionally rhapsodic nature nor its little internal rhythmical subtleties, but its departures from the diatonic norm to which he is accustomed in melody even more thoroughly than in harmony. He has been accustomed to tolerate a certain amount of melodic chromaticism by way of slither over a firm foundation of diatonic harmony (e.g. "O Star of Eve"). Indeed, slides of mere semitones themselves actually make a sickly appeal to many ears. We are tonally in the dark for a few moments but we are, literally, feeling our way step by step—and in a familiar room at that. It is the *leaps* in the dark—the so-called "augmented" and "diminished" intervals possible in the chromatic scale but almost completely foreign to the diatonic scale—that bother us and seem unmelodious.

And we must grant that the musical man-in-the-street's objection has a rational basis in instinctive feeling. These intervals, like the wide leaps often taken by the melodies of modern composers, are difficult, if not impossible, to *sing*. Though the listener is not called upon to sing such instrumental melodies as Ex. 20, he is instinctively conscious that they are not singable and hence that they are, to that extent, unnatural.* But since such melodies are not *intended* to be sung (usually) and can be played more or less comfortably on the instruments they are written for, there is no reason

---

* I have used the word "singable" in a rather loose way. A good many instrumental melodies in the older music are *unvocal*, even positively unsingable, as they stand. But they do not advertise their impossibility and the singing animal can easily, even unconsciously, provide himself mentally with a sort of singable simplification of the composer's idea. To take an elementary example: he can simplify the thirteenth mentioned above, in Beethoven's Op. 7, to a sixth.

why melody should remain, if not in a state of nature (whatever that was—for even folk-song is hardly that), at least fettered by the inhibitions of natural instinct. The horseman, the cyclist and the motorist have all acquired a set of muscular reflexes quite different from those of the "naturally" progressing pedestrian.* Why not the musician? And, of course, the cultured musician has done so long ago.

Whence have all these awkward intervals sprung? That question can only be answered by another: What are all melodic intervals derived from? To which the answer is, "Either from a scale or a chord," though that is an answer of expediency and is not historically accurate. A scale, as Dr. Dyson puts it,† is "an intellectual abstraction . . . a formula derived from the analysis of melody." And it is certain that man made tunes long before he made chords. Nevertheless, it is true that "natural" (i.e., sung) melody prefers steps to leaps and that examination of a tune reveals some definite path to which these steps have kept. And these few paths, trodden by the thousands of melodies men sang, are what we call scales. Some of the paths (the old modes) long fell into disuse, and the right of way

* And even walking must be considered a cultural acquirement if we began with swinging from tree to tree.

† *The New Music*.

appeared till recently to have lapsed; others (the pentatonic and other unusual scales) were used only by the
peasant musicians of Scotland, Russia, Hungary and
other backwaters of musical thought; but cultured
European music came to prefer two only—our familiar
major and minor. And once these paths were clearly
defined, composers consciously, but quite naturally,
kept to them—as one does keep to a field-path instead
of wandering at large.

Hence it is true to say that a great many, probably
the majority, of the melodies and melodic ideas (themes,
motives) of the great masters have been derived from
either the major or minor scale. And then again, as
instrumental music developed and drifted away from
its origin in song, the separate components of broken-
up chords (arpeggios) also provided basic material for
composers' imaginations to work on. So at least as early
as Bach we find plenty of examples (for instance, the
subject of the A flat Fugue, No. 17, in the first book of
the *Forty-eight*) of melodies derived from chords,
usually common chords or the more familiar discords.
A large number of Wagner's themes are actually derived from a single chord, the added sixth which we
discussed at such length in Chapter 2. Such chord-
built melodies hardly ever consist solely of the harmony
notes, however; the chords only provide a sort of skele-

ton to be filled out to a greater or lesser extent with passing-notes, usually tiny bits of scale. So that hybrid types of melody exist covering the whole range from pure chord-melody (like the "Sword" motif in the *Ring*) to pure scale-melody (such as "God Save the King"). And so it is correct, in an unhistoric sense, to say that all melody is derived from either a scale or a chord or both.

How does this help us to a better understanding of modern melody? Study of modern scales is not of much help since, as we have just seen, scales are only theoretical abstractions deduced from the practice of composers. When we say that the semitonal scale * is *the* modern scale *par excellence*, we only indicate that the composer demands perfect freedom to range where he likes, that (as far as he is concerned) footpaths no longer exist. But the opening up of all the *old* ways again has been interesting, though sometimes confusing. As a rule we find melodies written in such scales "difficult" in exact proportion to the divergence of the scale from the familiar major or minor. We soon ac-

* Most modern theorists prefer this term to the old name "chromatic scale." Others, from its twelve equal degrees, call it the "duodecuple scale." And there is a real difference. As its name implies, the old chromaticism was only a passing dab of twopenny color laid on the penny plain of diatonicism. Now that this scale has become a Thing-in-Itself, as the philosophers say, the term "chromatic" applied to it is meaningless.

custom ourselves to free modern use of the old modes.*
But when a composer like Bartók revives some scale
peculiar to Magyar folk-music (say, the pentatonic
scale, C, D, F sharp, G, A) we are likely to be badly
fogged.

And we also come across regrettable examples in
modern music of the cart being put before the horse
(or the egg coming before the hen), the theoretical abstraction being devised first and melodies concocted
"in" it afterwards. We have seen how the most important of these artificial scales—the whole-tone scale
—came into being. Rimsky-Korsakov invented another
of alternate whole-tones and semitones (though only
for a limited range of "fantastic" effects), and later
composers in a desperate effort to be original at all
costs have toyed with all sorts of weird and wonderful artificial scales.

There is essentially all the difference in the world
between such poseurs and sincere composers like Bartók, who we know has soaked himself so thoroughly
in his native folk-music that its peculiar scales have

* Though probably Walton, when he wrote that jolly tune in
E flat (with the flattened seventh) in the middle of *Portsmouth
Point*, did not give half a moment's thought to the Mixolydian
mode. The modal revival, at first dreadfully self-conscious, no
longer worries about itself and is now able to behave naturally and
spontaneously.

worn as deep grooves in his mind as the normal diatonic scales have done in our own. But unfortunately the results are so much alike that, both articles being so strange to us, we cannot in practice distinguish between the genuine and the artificial product. To return to the "path" metaphor: these artificial scales are paths leading nowhere, not naturally worn by the passing of generation after generation of wayfarers, but uselessly constructed by people with no goal who want to give the impression that they have a very special and individual one.

Confronted by a melody written in one of these unusual scales, the pianist has an invaluable resource denied to the mere passive listener—the very simple one of playing the scale itself a dozen times or so. (It would be better still to sing it.) Unfortunately the most "difficult" melodic lines in contemporary music are those related to no scale in the true sense. For the semitonal scale implies in practice the negation of scale, or at least the blotting out of scale values. Paths, with their individual characteristics, are obliterated; they all lie within this duodecuple field, but the modern composer of the atonal school wanders all over it without paying any attention to them. (And the quartertone people have got through the hedge, so to speak, into the next field.)

The clue to melody of this kind must be sought in modern harmony, not in the modern no-scale. Many an awkward scrap of melody turns out, on investigation, to be built of arpeggios, more or less decorated with passing notes, of new-formation chords. As usual, Holst will provide us with a clear and simple example. When we remember his fondness for the interweaving of common chords a semitone apart, even telescoping them into a single chord * as in Ex. 6, it is easy enough to recognize the apparently disjointed opening choral phrase of the scherzo of his *Choral Symphony:*—

EXAMPLE 23

Ev-er let the fan-cy roam, Pleas-ure nev-er is at home

(*Novello, London*)

as a simple, unadorned arpeggio of just such a telescoped chord (C, E, G and D flat, F, A flat). But only an ear that has grown accustomed to such chords and accepts them as comparatively consonant can find coherence

* Note for pedants: Even this *can* be "explained" as what old-fashioned theorists called a fundamental discord, an unusual form of the minor thirteenth:-

EXAMPLE 22

though it is quite obvious that Holst never thought of it as such.

(what the average listener would consider genuine
"melodiousness") in melodies derived from them. Be-
sides, melodies like Ex. 23, based on simple, unadorned
arpeggios, are rare; and the ornamental passing-notes,
though they may help to smooth out angularities, do
not make intelligent recognition any easier. Incidentally, those melodic lines in Scriabin's later music which
appear to be based on the whole-tone scale, with
chromatic passing-notes, are really to be explained harmonically in this way, i.e., as decorated arpeggios of
his complicated artificial chords. Naturally, the apparent melodiousness of such melodies usually varies in
proportion to the degree of dissonance of the chords
they are derived from.

The only cases where the duodecuple scale is of any
help to the understanding of atonal melody are those
where the melody is not merely written "in" the scale,
but actually based "on" it. In this example from Hindemith's *Tanzstück*, Op. 37, No. 4:—

EXAMPLE 24

(*Associated Music Publishers, New York*)

the backbone of the melody is the chromatic descent
from F sharp to A flat. The A in the first measure is
a decorative addition to, just as the F sharp instead of
the expected D natural in measure three is a decorative
variation of the scale. The substitution of F sharp, G
for B flat, A in the fourth measure (*rising* chromatically
to the climactic A flat, instead of continuing the descent
to it) is a slightly more elaborate variation, but the
chromatic scale is the obvious foundation of the whole
thing. But this is merely the old "Star of Eve" slither,
disguised by the little trimmings I have pointed out
and with the solid ground of diatonic harmony cut
from under its feet. (I have purposely quoted the melody without its background.) Still, because the melody
feels its way step by step and straight ahead (for it
only *pretends* to leap sideways into the dark unknown),
it is fairly easy to accept it. Play the descending chromatic scale from F sharp to A flat a few times first, and
you will find that the tune begins to sound as natural as
"God Save the King."

I may say that in putting forward this "explanation" of (or way of looking at) Hindemith's tune, I
do not suggest that it is the only one—any more than
I suggest that the tune itself is a good one. The theme
might be regarded even more plausibly, though more
banally, as a chromatic descent from F sharp to B

natural, answered by a chromatic ascent to the same note from the lower F sharp. But that in no way affects the truth of my remarks. In either case the chromatic scale is the backbone of the melody and, once the ear has recognized that, it easily accepts the trimmings because they are only deviations from an unmistakable straight line.

To hear sense in the sort of melody that consists of ornamented arpeggios of unfamiliar modern chords is infinitely more difficult. The average listener cannot distinguish between essential and decorative notes. And if, in addition, he is baffled by rhythmic subtleties and can distinguish neither phrase periods nor pivoting points in the melody—all the things that make melody articulate—he has every excuse for denying that it is melody at all. Or, if he is broad-minded enough to admit that it *is*, in intention, melody of a sort, for denying it every trace of meaning or coherence. And as far as he is concerned, he is perfectly right; it *is* incoherent nonsense to his ear and mind, just as the preface to *Back to Methuselah* (to say nothing of Joyce's *Ulysses* in another way and T. S. Eliot's *The Waste Land* in a third) would have been to a cultured English monk of Chaucer's day. But the fact that it is meaningless and incoherent to a mind and ear in the defective state of culture of his own does not give him the right to deny its sense absolutely and to denounce the composer as an impostor and all who do understand him as dupes or pretentious humbugs. He has ample excuse for being wrong himself, but a perfect excuse for being wrong does not prove that one is right. . . . All of which is too obvious to be worth pointing out but that it is completely ignored by about 87½ per cent of our musical people, professional and amateur.

"Well," someone may object, "I admit that by accustoming my ear to new chords and new-old scales I may possess myself of a key to the sense of these spiky, ejaculatory lines which so many contemporary composers want us to accept as melodies. But do not melodies like these, which can only be appreciated by an intellectual process, differ radically from all that we have hitherto considered melody? One hasn't to 'understand' a melody by Mozart or Chopin or Wagner. The old melody was a natural, spontaneous result of some more or less emotional excitement of the composer's mind, naturally and spontaneously inducing a sort of reflection of the excitement in the listener. Conscious thought never entered into the matter. But now everything is calculated, cold-blooded and unnatural," and so on in the same strain *ad nauseam*.

To which the reply is: firstly, that melody never has really been as naïvely spontaneous as all this except in the most primitive folk-music; and secondly, that the ordinary major and minor scales cannot be considered *a priori* more fit for the expression of natural, spontaneous ideas than any other. Ideas may occur spontaneously in terms of any musical idiom to which the composer is thoroughly accustomed. And, as I have already remarked, even the average modern composer is still more accustomed, in his subconscious depths, to diatonicism than to anything else. But it is only to be expected that ideas will occur spontaneously in the new idiom to those composers who have sufficiently saturated their minds in it. The ideas may be good or bad, just as diatonic ideas may be good or bad. They *may* be merely manufactured. Probably they often are by the mountebanks we cannot yet clearly distinguish from the genuine pioneers. But have not thousands of diatonic melodies also been merely manufactured?

A listener with his mind equally steeped in the idiom of some very advanced composer will naturally apprehend the shape of his melodies and be immediately moved by them, without any intervention of the intellect, just as you and I "feel" a Bach fugue subject. The intellectual effort is necessary only when there is a gap of common understanding to be bridged. To use the well-worn "language" metaphor once more, the intellectual effort is precisely equivalent to that which one has to make continually in reading a foreign language one knows only imperfectly. Instead of thinking directly in the language, as you do if you know it thoroughly, you have consciously to *translate* all the time. And this intellectual operation intervenes persistently between the writer's thought and your grasp of it, befogging even prosaic ideas and utterly destructive of poetic magic.

But the writer's compatriots have to make no such effort; and in your own case, as your knowledge of the language increases, the intervention of the conscious mind becomes less and less necessary till finally you discover that, like a native, you are getting along without it altogether. If you don't understand German at all well, you will prefer Marlowe's Faust to Goethe's. But no Englishman is quite such a fool as to suppose that English is the only natural language and that poetry in a foreign language he does not understand is mere gibberish, or at any rate "cold-blooded, unnatural and purely a product of the intellect." He *might* justifiably think that of Esperanto, or Ido, or Volapuk poetry. But poets don't write in Esperanto, though verse-makers may amuse themselves with it. And a little experience will soon show that it is not quite so difficult as it seems at first to sort out the Esperantists and the genuine foreigners among modern composers.

6

FORM AND SPIRIT

IN discussing the alleged incoherence and admittedly rhapsodic nature of much modern melody I have purposely omitted all mention of a factor that has done a great deal to produce this effect of incoherence— the abandonment of repetition and sequence. But the matter belongs properly not to the sphere of melody alone but to the general structure of modern music, its *form* and the spirit of which it is the embodiment. Even the abandonment of repetition and sequence, though apparently the most radical of all our modern musical revolutions, is only the logical continuation of an evolutionary tendency that can be traced through the art-music of the last hundred and fifty years. But here again, of course, it is arguable that art has nothing to do with strict logic, that its evolution proceeds by cycles rather than in straight lines, and that the logical continuation of a tendency in a rigid straight line is the equivalent of flying off at an intellectual tangent.

Everyone who knows anything at all about music knows that the simplest forms of musical structure are built up by the contrasting and repeating of simple, well-defined phrases. Phrase A is followed by the contrasting phrase B and so on; and perhaps A, or a slight modification of it, is finally repeated to round the thing off. There are all sorts of complications and elaborations of the idea, and its development has resulted in turn in classical sonata-form and in such elaborations of the latter as we find in the first movements of Elgar's symphonies on the one hand and Scriabin's *Prometheus* on the other. Statement—contrast—repetition: the idea seems to be the essence of all coherent musical structure from the most primitive to the most complicated.

But to return for a moment to simple melody: it is evident that a melody built in this simple way, beautiful as it may be, is not a very lofty type of organism. Even the contrasts are usually only repetitions-with-a-difference (as in "God Save the King," for instance); so that, essentially, one idea—the first phrase—has been eked out to the size of four. And composers, who could easily learn by rule of thumb this art of eking out, found things very easy for them. As Mr. Shaw put it in *The Perfect Wagnerite*, "given the first line of 'Pop

Goes the Weasel,' or 'Yankee Doodle,' any musical cobbler could supply the remaining three." Everyone will agree that, whether or not it needed a Schubert to invent the first four bars of "Die Forelle," it certainly needed no Schubert to follow them up with the next four. Any student could have done it as well.

The first upward step of simple metrical melody is taken when the composer, instead of "cobbling" his contrasting phrase, is fortunate enough to find that his creative imagination is still working at full pressure and so is able to produce a *natural* continuation of his opening, as Mozart and Beethoven did in "Dove sono" and the slow movement of the Fifth Symphony. Here already we are more than half way to Wagner's "continuous melody," a definitely higher type. Symmetry, half living thought, half padding, gradually makes way for rhapsody, vital at every point in the line. There is a loss in clarity and simplicity of outline, but a gain in cutting away the superfluous. Wagner's rhapsodic melodies at their best have nothing superfluous. They are throughout closely packed with thought—a concentration, as it were, of everything vital in the old type of melody.

But there is still an element of repetition—mainly, of course, *varied* repetition—even in Wagner's "endless melody," repetition not of phrases but of motives. The

rhapsodic line tends to become a sequence of certain
patterns:—

EXAMPLE 25

But Schoenberg and his disciples have eliminated even
this amount of repetition. They regard sequences as
mere inflation, the equivalent of verbosity in speech.
They want to do away with the last traces of the superfluous; the single statement should be enough. Not that
their practice is always strictly in accordance with
their theorizing, but their theories do explain the extremely elliptical nature of much of their music.

But does all this excuse the apparent incoherence of
their utterance? Is not their argument fallacious in that
it is based too exclusively on the imperfect parallel between music and speech? A musical statement *is* of a
different nature from a verbal one. Musical statements
are linked in a pattern arising from their own shapes
and cannot be linked in any other way. Verbal statements are linked in an argument by the *sense* of the
words, not by the words themselves. But music has

no sense outside itself, except in so far as we ourselves like to give it such. Is it not arguable that by doing away with repetition and symmetry in the unfolding of their musical patterns, these Central European musicians have destroyed the only bond of coherence music can have and are turning out music that is, in essence, as disconnected as a page from a dictionary?

It is useless to try to give an absolute answer to these questions, since one's answers must depend entirely on one's conception of the very nature of music. But nine hundred and ninety-eight out of every thousand musicians would probably answer without hesitation that music so concise and elliptical as this is actually, not merely apparently, incoherent. But they would be on surer ground if they contented themselves with pointing out that, in any case, the game is not worth the candle. And this seems to be the truth of the matter. Shavian He-Ancients and Nietzschean Supermen may be able to listen with pleasure to music so condensed, so tightly packed with meaning—by which, of course, I mean purely musical meaning—but it seems hardly likely that human beings at our own stage of evolutionary development will ever do so.

The little group of over-intellectual composers who have carried this elimination of expansion and repetition to an extreme is too small and too little accepted by the musical world in general for it to be necessary to say anything more about this tendency in the exaggerated form they practice. But the tendency itself is common to all composers who are genuinely modern in spirit. It shows itself most clearly in the field of musical architecture, "form" as we call it. While the modern composer usually recognizes still the necessity for formal balance, he no longer thinks it necessary (as Holst, I think, once put it) to "hang up your grandmother's portrait on one side of the mantelpiece because you have your grandfather's on the other." The old idea that structural balance was largely a matter of counting measures arose no doubt from the analogy of phrase-balance, but it rested on the false assumption that music exists in space like a picture, instead of in time like a poem. And it has been able to survive so long because musicians unfortunately study music on paper with the eye far more than they do in actual performance with the ear. But that symmetry which was obtained by wholesale repetitions was really only a conventional, though convenient, fiction—and modern practice refuses to recognize it as anything else.

Nothing, therefore, is more abhorrent to the modern composer than the practice of singing his song twice over. His first fine careless rapture has to suffice for us; we must take it or leave it. (After all, the old custom of repeating the exposition section of a symphonic first movement was often merely a sop to the lazy-minded, and modern conductors, when they omit the repeat out of respect to the more wide-awake audiences of to-day, who would be bored by such tautology, are simply bowing to the prevalent feeling.) * But a malicious critic might object that it is simply the absence of "careless rapture" which is at the bottom of this desire for curtness and condensation. The true lyrical impulse is expansive. It has to be curbed, certainly; a man in love with the music he is making will go on for ever, as Schubert often did—that delightfullest of bores. Let us have compression, by all means. But we like to feel the pressure of the force that is held in check. The modern composer cannot be as naïve as Schubert or Browning's thrush, but he does seem at times to have gone pretty dismally to the other extreme. In his denunciation of the old romantic "rapture" (or "rhetoric" as he contemptuously calls it) he has partially confounded that unique excitement, partly emotional, partly intellectual, which is the vital essence of so much great music, with the sonorous flatulence of

* Admittedly, the repeat is *sometimes* indispensable (e.g., in the first movement of Beethoven's *Pathétique* Sonata) and cannot be omitted without barbarous butchery. But only too often the repeat was mere "composer's routine."

the later romantic composers, "intoxicated with the exuberance of their own verbosity," the excitement of the first movement of the *Eroica* with the excitement of *Ein Heldenleben*. And, for good or ill, this type of excitement is replaced in a great deal of modern music by quite a different force.

In practically all the music of the past the driving impulse—what I have called the "excitement"—has been the tendency in the composer's mind to generate shapes from shapes, a clumsy expression which is the best I can find to describe a subtle and peculiar process. Given a scrap of melody, the mind of a fertile composer is beset with continuations of it—answering phrases, sequential developments of the phrase or part of the phrase, and so on—all clamoring more or less urgently to be used. One musical shape springs from another, naturally and inevitably if he is what we call "inspired," or helped out by the obstetric processes of technique if he is not. These fluid shapes spread themselves over the solid basis of a rhythmical (or rather metrical) framework, and so rhythm gives shape and physical vitality to the whole. But the *entraînement* of the music is "emotional-intellectual." In the new music rhythm replaces this excitement as the actual driving-power, rhythm and meter infinitely more subtle than we find them in the older music, rhythm organized with terrific nervous intensity. In this respect Stravin-sky's *Petrushka* and *Sacre du Printemps* on the one hand * and jazz on the other seem to have been the prototypes.

These modern rhythms are freer than the rhythms of nineteenth-century music in that they break away much further and more persistently from the simple, rather square patterns which music acquired from song (lyric poetry) and dance. But they are not free in the sense that they are the result of a mere breaking of bonds, of license taken to meander at will. There *are* plenty of examples in twentieth-century music of rhythms "free" in this negative sense. The Piano Sonata mentioned in the footnote on page 62 is a case in point. But they are infrequent in music which is genuinely modern in feeling. In *that* the irregularities are usually organized and often recur in more or less regular pat-terns. Take one of the most popular of modern British orchestral pieces, Walton's *Portsmouth Point*. Walton disdains neither diatonic tunes nor sequential construc-tion, but the driving impulse in his overture is purely *rhythmic*. Block-chords, terse, flying counterpoint (slightly *Meistersinger*-ish counterpoint), orchestral

* A good deal of the music of the older Russian composers, other than Tchaikovsky, owes much more to purely rhythmic impetus and less to force of logic or emotional excitement than that of their Western contemporaries.

color—all these are hardly more than media for the embodiment of rhythm. Take the opening bars:—

EXAMPLE 26

(*Oxford University Press*)

Comment is unnecessary. Even the melodies are far more important rhythmically than as regards curve:—

EXAMPLE 27

(*Oxford University Press*)

And here is a comparable, indeed still more pertinent, example from an American work, the first movement of Walter Piston's Second Symphony:

EXAMPLE 28

(*Arrow Music Press*)

Instead of shape begetting shape as in the older music, rhythm now begets rhythm. In place of the sequence of line and the sequence of emotion we have rhythmic sequence. The driving power is physical in nature, rather than emotional or intellectual.

But we must remember that that verdict is not as condemnatory as it may appear to some; that is, to those who assume without further reflection that the physical is necessarily more primitive ("lower," as they would probably put it) than the intellectual or emotional. To begin with, all art worth calling art has a strong primitive element in it. We need another word here; "crude" will serve. The rhythmic appeal of a fox-trot or a military march or Ravel's *Bolero* is crude. So is the emotional appeal of the "Hallelujah" Chorus or "Home, Sweet Home" or Liszt's only too well-known *Liebestraum*. So is the intellectual appeal of pieces of simple imitation such as delighted generations of maiden aunts and churchwardens in "All we, like sheep." And even crudity is not always bad. But there is nothing crude about the rhythmic verve of *Portsmouth Point* or Piston's melody. The new predominance of rhythm is a downward step only in the sense that the simple-melodic-with-harmonic-background style of Haydn and his contemporaries was a descent from the polyphonic style of the generation before. Musicians concentrate from time to time on some aspect of their material hitherto considered to be of only secondary importance—in the eighteenth century the vertical, as opposed to the horizontal, way of looking at musical texture, at the present time, rhythm—and for a while give it precedence over all other elements. It is only a form of the familiar tendency to glorify Cinderella.

And this glorification of rhythm is symptomatic of a tendency which, more than any other, is the mark of what most keen observers agree in considering the truly modern spirit in music—the tendency to think wholly in terms of sound instead of partly in terms of literature or painting. The music which we feel to be modern in spirit as well as in substance is "pure" music. Even when a composer's point of departure is literary or pictorial, as Walton's is in the piece we have just been discussing, he usually leaves it at once without so much as a backward glance. Honegger's *Pacific 231* (if we decline to dismiss it as a mere clever technical exercise, like Strauss's sheep) is almost an isolated instance in modern music of deliberate tone-painting, though even here the composer really contents himself with extracting a few elements of rhythmic suggestion from his subject and building up his piece independently on *them*. But then *Pacific 231* is not only an exception but a piece of rather bad music, quite unworthy of the man who wrote the String Quartet in C minor. As for Mossolov's once well-advertised *Iron Foundry*, it is nakedly and unashamedly lyrical, a simple tune with an accompaniment—but unfortunately not a very good tune and with a singularly unpleasant accompaniment, in fact the precise aesthetic equivalent of Sullivan's "Chorister" in terms of modern harmony and modern orchestra.

The vague emotional program is quite as unfashionable as the definite literary one. The modern romanticists, like Arnold Bax, who still toy with it are so few in number that one is tempted to deny that they are really modernists at all. Which is absurd, of course. Nevertheless, Bax's music has little more than Elgar's, and no more than Delius's, in common with that which we recognize as truly modern. Bax's tendency to wealth of expression, to soaring on the wings of emotional rhetoric, his underlying romanticism of thought—all these are the antitheses of the fashions of modernism.

Like Delius, another modernist in harmony only, he is a romantic who has acquired a subtler technique from the impressionists. Sibelius, who began as a romantic of the Bax type and remained one till about the period of his Fourth Symphony, is much nearer to the modernist spirit, in spite of the fact that he bothers very little about harmonic innovations as such. But his severe economy of texture, his drastic elimination of inessentials in structure and his avoidance of rhetorical expansion brings him nearer to the Waltons and Hindemiths than Bax is, for all the modernity of his harmonies.

To say that, of course, implies no reproach to Bax and the other contemporary practitioners of romanticism, with their keen eyes for landscape and its spiritual values and their ears pricked to catch the echoes of old legend. Many people would regard it as a compliment to them. It is all a matter of taste. But when we speak of modernism in this sense we only imply—we can only imply—prevalent taste, fashion. The modern romantics are not in the fashion. We may leave it at that, adding only that their music presents few real problems (other than harmonic ones at times) to anyone with a reasonably wide knowledge of musical processes in general and a mind broad enough to accept liberal and highly individual interpretations of the old architectural conventions.

7

A NOTE ON THE TWELVE-
TONE SYSTEM

TWENTY years ago the "twelve-tone system," as distinguished from the twelve-tone scale, was employed only by a tiny handful of Central European composers—by its inventor, Josef Matthias Hauer, and by Arnold Schoenberg and his pupils, such as Alban Berg and Anton von Webern. But the system appears now to have taken root; it is constantly referred to in articles and discussions on modern music.

Earlier in this book certain weaknesses in atonal music were discussed, but no mention was made there of the device adopted to combat them. These weaknesses were stated on pages 85, 96, and 97: "The semitonal scale implies in practice the blotting out of scale values" (in other words, no degree of the scale has any special function of relationship to any of the others) and the elimination of repetition and sequence in the melodic line has "destroyed the only bond of coherence music can have." Without some sort of artificial backbone, in short, atonal music is unpleasantly like jelly. Schoenberg found this artificial backbone in Hauer's idea of "tone-rows," an idea that naturally appealed to a composer whose music showed an increasing tendency towards the excessively intellectual.

What *is* this idea, then? Briefly, this. The composer takes the twelve notes of the chromatic scale and arranges them in any order he likes, say: C sharp (or D flat), A, B, G, A flat (or G sharp), F sharp (or G flat), A sharp (or B flat), D, E, E flat (or D sharp), C, F. This "tone-row" then provides the sole basis of the particular movement or composition. The intervals may be inverted, in this case becoming C sharp, F, E flat, G, F sharp, A flat, E, C, B flat, B, D, A. And both the original row and the inversion may be played backwards: F, C, E flat, E, D, etc. and A, D, B, B flat, C, E, etc., or even transposed. And any of these may begin in the middle (on the same principle as cutting a pack of cards, which doesn't alter the sequence of the cards). But all the notes in the row, or in the derivation from the row, must be used in the settled order each time before the row may be repeated.

Let us see how this works in practice. Consider the first four measures of the Waltz from Schoenberg's *Five Piano Pieces*, Op. 23, written in 1923, one of the first compositions in which he employed twelve-tone rows:

EXAMPLE 29

(*Wilhelm Hansen, Copenhagen*)

The right-hand part gives the basic tone-row of the whole piece, the same row that I gave as my example. You will notice that the left-hand part consists of the same row, but beginning with the sixth note (I have numbered each note in the row to simplify matters) and with two or three notes sounded simultaneously as chords instead of being spread out consecutively as a melody. Similarly the mere notes of the next five measures, as apart from their rhythm and duration, can be shown simply by the figures without using music-type at all:

Right Hand	7 6 8 10	11 12 4	6 7 8		2	5
			3			
Left Hand	9	1 5		9 10	12 1 3	4 6 7 8
		2			11	

Before you sweepingly condemn this as mere mathematics (and a rather childish form of mathematics at that), consider its undeniable advantages as an artificial backbone for atonal music. Though scale values still no longer exist, each degree of the scale now again has a definite relationship to the rest—if only for the duration of that particular piece. Transposition of the row provides a substitute for modulation. And the row does supply a bond of coherence, a very rigid bond, that performs the function of the old melodic links of simple repetition and sequence. Further, it contrives to do this without the slightest concession to the old key-principle; for, as every note in the twelve-tone scale is heard an equal number of times in each piece, none can predominate and form a sort of shadow keynote as sometimes happened in the earlier essays in atonalism. Whereas the beginnings of atonalism were purely anarchistic, the twelve-tone system enforces the most rigid communism.

The obvious criticism of the system is that such music is purely intellectual, purely "paper" music. In this rigid and uncompromising form, perhaps it is. But in the hands of Schoenberg's most gifted pupil, Alban Berg, the twelve-tone system has produced remarkable results.

Berg generally uses it with very considerable license,

however. He does not ascetically renounce all note-repetition; he does not keep rigidly to the true order of the row; he even slips in occasional notes here and there that do not belong to the row at all. And through this freedom he achieves music that, however strange to many people's ears, is at least human, expressive and by no means incomprehensible to the practiced ear. Let us look for a moment or two at a couple of examples from Berg's last composition, the Violin Concerto.

To begin with, the row of notes on which the entire Concerto is based is not a mere dry, crabbed line, like the right-hand part of Ex. 29. It consists of the series: G, B flat, D, F sharp, A, C, E, G sharp, B, C sharp, E flat, F. Try it over on the piano and you will find it has a much more friendly sound than the Schoenberg example. In fact notes 1, 2 and 3, and 5, 6 and 7 from it form ordinary minor common chords, while 3, 4, 5 and 7, 8, 9 provide major chords; even the most foreign-sounding part of the row—9, 10, 11, 12 —is only a fragment of whole-tone scale. And if you invert the row or play it backwards it still sounds quite normal and comprehensible.

Now let us see how Berg uses this row in practice. Take this two-measure excerpt that opens the *allegretto* section of the first movement:

EXAMPLE 30

(*Universal Edition, Vienna*)

(The right-hand part is really played by two clarinets; the left-hand by pizzicato strings.) The first measure consists of the notes of the row transposed so as to begin on D; the second measure consists of the inversion of the row transposed so as to begin on A. It will be noticed that Berg indulges in deliberate note-repetition and uses one or two notes quite out of the proper order.

Particularly interesting is the way in which Berg contrives to reconcile the twelve-tone system with the diatonic tunes he weaves into the score: an Austrian folk-tune and a Bach chorale. Take the first entry of the chorale on the solo violin:

EXAMPLE 31

(*Universal Edition, Vienna*)

The first two measures consist of the row transposed to begin on F sharp (which is actually played in its simple form by the bassoon); the identity of the first four notes of the Bach with the last four of the row is turned to account very cunningly. The remainder of the quotation consists of the row transposed to begin on B flat. Again notes are repeated or used irregularly.

I have already emphasized the ease with which "ideas may occur spontaneously in terms of any musical idiom to which the composer is thoroughly accustomed . . . the fact that a very little familiarity with a new harmonic system is sufficient to set a man's fancy playing with it, just as it normally plays with the everyday elements of diatonic scales and arpeggios of familiar chords in the invention of melodies." *

That is obviously what happened in Berg's case. And I was once assured by a well-known English composer that, after a long period of lying fallow and sympathetic study of twelve-tone music, he suddenly began to compose again in a time of emotional stress and found

* See pages 47 and 91.

himself spontaneously working in terms of this apparently over-intellectual system.

But English and American twelve-tone composers nearly always tend to follow the example of Berg rather than of Schoenberg at his strictest. They take all kinds of liberties. They get hints from twelve-tone technique without employing it systematically. Or they mingle twelve-tone with other chromatic idioms, as Debussy sometimes used to mix whole-tone elements into music that was otherwise more normal. Samuel Barber, for instance, in the slow movement of his Piano Sonata, sets a twelve-tone accompaniment figure going and then puts over it non-twelve-tonal arabesque melodies in more or less "normal" harmonic relation to it at any given point:

EXAMPLE 32

(*Schirmer, New York*)

What is the ordinary listener to make of all this? His solution in this case is the one that I have insisted on throughout this little book: the gaining of familiarity. Admittedly that is no easy business, for very little not-too-difficult twelve-tone piano music has (as far as I am aware) been written so far. But Křenek's *Twelve Short Piano Pieces*, Op. 83 (Schirmer) is admirable for this purpose, and you will find that to play over a few times the row on which Ex. 29 is based will make even the strange piece from which it is taken sound a little less enigmatic. And so with any other twelve-tone piece you can lay hands on; your real problem is to accustom your ear to the row—pronounce it which way you like.

But it is a flinty path that you will have to tread and at the end of it you are always liable to find Tony Weller's charity boy chuckling at you.

8

FASHIONS IN MODERN MUSIC

ONE of the major difficulties that confront the layman in his attempt to make friends with contemporary music is its many-sideness. As I remarked in an earlier chapter, the most important additions to the musical vocabulary during the last half-century have been made "by a number of minor composers whose contributions have been curiously different"; the innovations have come not only in bewildering quantity but from very different directions. There is not one "modern music"; there are a number of "modern musics," some differing from each other as much as from the classical-romantic music we are all familiar with. Evolutionary, revolutionary, reactionary—some are mutually exclusive, canceling each other out. Sometimes, on the other hand, very different, apparently antagonistic tendencies have coalesced or cross-fertilized each other. Eclectic composers have taken one conception from one movement, all sorts of technical hints from another, and harnessed them to an aesthetic ideal borrowed from a third. And that sort of eclecticism is not necessarily a sign of creative weakness, nor are its products invariably feeble affairs of patchwork. There is good eclecticism as well as bad; most of the very greatest composers of the past have been eclectics, drawing from many sources but welding all they have drawn into something new and personal; and during the last fifteen years or so, especially, there has been a marked tendency for most of the leading composers who are truly "contemporary" in spirit to draw on the common stock of new technical devices and idioms contributed by practically all the earlier innovators of the century, and to use them (may we put it?) with their sharper edges worn down by rubbing against each other. Bartók, greatest of them all, is the outstanding example of such a latter-day eclectic.

These various tendencies, almost as numerous and changeable as feminine fashions, have flowed from all kinds of origins: from individual theories, from the personal idioms of outstanding composers, from national leanings, from general aesthetic currents of the day, even from governmental pressure. It may be of some help to map out roughly the general course of these currents during the first half of this century, to see how they have crossed and affected each other and are now at last beginning to mingle in a common stream.

First of all, let us look back for a moment to the beginning of this century—for almost all genuinely modern music, of whatever kind, represents a reaction in technique and aesthetic ideal against the favorite techniques and valued ideals of the nineteenth and early twentieth centuries. During the first ten or fifteen years of this century, it is true, a certain amount of music that is modern in the sense that it is "difficult" in idiom was produced in the course of efforts to push nineteenth-century techniques to their furthest possible extreme; but even the composers who were doing this either died or were affected in some way by the new ideals.

Perhaps the most important fact to be grasped is that these "new" ideals were really quite old ones. Our general notions of music are still so shaped and conditioned by the music of the nineteenth century, which is most familiar to us, that we tend to think of its essential qualities as qualities essential to *all* music. And by far the highest common factor of practically all nineteenth-century music is human, personal emotion. The music exists in order to communicate to us what the composer has felt: lofty aspiration, patriotic fervor, longing for a beloved woman, suicidal gloom. . . . Now that is all very fascinating; the desire to communicate personal emotions through music produced a wonderful crop of masterpieces and (among other things) enormously enlarged the technical resources of the art. It was a historical phase that music was bound to pass through, and it was an exhilarating phase. But it was only a phase. The expression of personal emotion, or even emotion of any kind, is not an essential function of music. Until the nineteenth century, until the so-called Age of Romanticism, emotional expression was usually a by-product of the act of musical composition—often a very minor one, even non-existent. The first concern of a composer of the earlier centuries was impeccable craftsmanship. He wrote for, and wanted to be judged by, his peers even though in the service of a prince or a church. During the decades preceding the advent of the Romantic era, the composer constructed a piece of music for use in church, or for people to dance to or for people to sing or play or listen to as an agreeable sound, idiomatically suitable for the medium of expression. If he set words to music, he tried to make his music reflect the mood of the words—not to express *his* mood at that moment. If he wrote music for the lyric stage, he depicted emotions with the help of music —but he did it as an actor does, or as a novelist who describes or reveals in dialogue what his characters are feeling. His own personal emotions at a given moment may have happened to coincide with the emotion it was his job to depict, but that was only accidental; otherwise his emotions, his personality, mattered to him only as a reservoir of experience. He had experienced joys or sorrow, and so he could convincingly depict joys or sorrow in a generalized way if necessary. Often it was not necessary at all. When Bach wrote the great G minor Fugue for organ or Mozart the *Jupiter* Symphony, neither was concerned with the expression or description or communication of emotion; he was concerned only with the construction of a piece of music. If these works, or any passages in them, seem to us to express definite emotions, that expressive element is incidental or accidental or even the mere product of our own imagining. Beethoven glorifying the heroic in general (or specifically Napoleon) in a symphony or thinking of the music of the spheres in the slow movement of the second *Razumovsky* Quartet is another matter. Mendelssohn working up his travel impressions of Holyrood Palace and the Hebrides in the *Scottish* Symphony and the *Fingal's Cave* Overture, Schumann embodying the musical record of a lonely, love-sick evening in the last movement of his *Fantasie*, Op. 17, Wagner sublimating a love-affair in *Tristan* and caricaturing a hostile music-critic in *Die Meistersinger,* Tchaikovsky pouring out his hopeless yearnings and neurotic fantasies in his Fifth and Sixth Symphonies: all these are even more personal, each representing a further stage in the inflation of the personal element in music.

But this inflation of the personal element has been found very distasteful, sometimes quite nauseating, by many twentieth-century musicians—including most of the leading composers. For good or ill, modern taste prefers the pre-romantic, pre-Beethovenian attitude of simple craftsmanship. The fashion affects our attitude even to the older masters; Beethoven is not the idol of modern composers, and no intelligent musician nowadays would dream of hailing J. S. Bach as a forerunner of romanticism, as was done forty or fifty years ago. The modern composer often feels an affinity with Bach, but with Bach the superb master of his craft, not with the emotional caricature of Bach we are still sometimes offered in the concert-hall.

Naturally the nineteenth-century ideals did not disappear suddenly; they were carried into the early twentieth century and developed to their furthest extreme by such masters as Richard Strauss, Mahler, Scriabin and the early Schoenberg. At first the main counter-influence came from Debussy, whose music is at least concerned with sensation instead of emotion (and hence often with the sensation of pure sound for its own sake) and renounces the expansive rhetoric of late romanticism. Beside him stood the younger and lesser figure of another Frenchman, Ravel, even more "classical" in feeling, much more the exponent of pure craftsmanship for its own sake. Debussy and Ravel to some extent rivaled and paced each other, and certainly influenced each other, and by the time Debussy died in 1918 he had abandoned the rendering of extra-musical sensations and was concerned with an art of pure sound.

But side by side with Debussy and Ravel, before the First World War, there were other if less pronounced indications that the tide was flowing against romanticism. In England the leading young composers evaded personal emotional expression by studying folk-song and basing their compositions on it; not in a spirit of patriotic excitement but because the English folk-tunes seemed so deliciously cool and simple and impersonally beautiful by comparison with the turgid heat of late romanticism. Sibelius, beginning as a romantic, subjected the romantic idiom itself to a highly individual process of cooling and drying and compression, hardening the texture, cutting out the rhetorical expansion. In Germany Reger sought to stiffen and intellectualize the romantic idiom with the aid of Bachian counterpoint. By the time the First World War broke out, musical romanticism was all but extinct. Mahler was dead, Scriabin had finished his life-work (he died the next year, 1915), even Strauss had begun to play with eighteenth-century pastiche and much reduced orchestral forces. Most important of all, Schoenberg had revolted from rhetorical expansion to an intensely compressed utterance and was already seeking ways and means of restoring bone and sinew to the amorphous jellylike mass which had resulted from *Tristan*-esque chromaticism developed to its last extremity. In his *Pierrot Lunaire* (1912), which might not unfairly be described as a piece of overripe romanticism gone rotten, he had introduced all sorts of rigid structural devices—themes played backward or with intervals reversed—which he was afterwards to employ wholesale in his "twelve-tone technique." * And this aspect of his music has often been misunderstood, not only by laymen but by professional musicians—who have also misunderstood the purpose of the intellectual ingenuities of Bachian counterpoint. "You can't hear all these reversals and inversions," it is objected. To which the answer is that you aren't expected or intended to. They are means of constructing music and the composer no more expects you to hear them than the architect of a

* As described on page 109.

building expects you to see his foundations and his steel girders and what not. Only in modern music of this kind and in truly modern architecture, there is no special effort to disguise the structure, no false shame expressed in false ornament.

A more serious criticism of this kind of music is that, even more seriously than romantic music, it lacks rhythmic vitality. But just as the clear-cut, rhythmical and colorful music of the Russian "nationalists" had in the late nineteenth century been greeted in the West as a welcome contrast to the heaviness and turgidity of even the greatest German romantics, there now appeared a brilliant pupil of one of these same nationalists (Rimsky-Korsakov)—Igor Stravinsky—who had absorbed a great deal of the harmonic and other idioms of Debussy, Scriabin and others, and combined them in his own earlier ballets—*The Fire Bird*, *Petrushka*, *Le Sacre du Printemps* (all pre-1914)—with the national Russian characteristics of bright sonority and vital rhythm. In so far as nineteenth-century musical nationalism was itself a phase of romanticism, these early Stravinsky ballets may also be regarded as final manifestations of the romantic age; for very soon afterward Stravinsky, exiled in Western Europe, also turned to the ideals of neo-classicism—even excluding the "too emotionally expressive" stringed instruments from several works written during 1920–24.

That exclusion of strings was an extreme measure, of course. But the nineteen-twenties, particularly the early nineteen-twenties, were a period of extreme measures, of feverish experiment in all directions, when the human ear was being taxed in one direction and puzzled in another by innovators who excitedly pursued their own methods of enlarging the language of music, often with very little regard for what others were doing. In Paris the little group of young musicians nicknamed by a journalist in 1920 "Les Six"—Honegger, Milhaud, Poulenc, Auric, Durey and Tailleferre—sought to realize their anti-romantic ideal of simple, clear, concise music by taking hints from the music-hall song, from Stravinsky and from the then newly fashionable American jazz; deliberate simplicity of melody and texture was piquantly perverted by the combination of two or more keys simultaneously. In 1923 Schoenberg arrived at *his* solution of the problem of no key at all: his twelve-tone technique. In 1922 a younger German, Paul Hindemith, emerged with a less frightening form of atonal neo-classicism; he too wished to get rid of romantic emotion, to write music that was first and foremost to be useful and used (*Gebrauchsmusik*), and which (although keyless and strongly dissonant) bustled along under the double rhythmic influences of jazz and the Bachian type of instrumental concerto with its incessant note-patterns. In Prague the Moravian Alois Hába began at the same time to experiment first with quarter-tones, later with still more minute intervals ("microtones"), a system on which he published a book in 1927. In America Henry Cowell compiled tremendous "tone-clusters" of all the notes on the piano that can be sounded simultaneously with the flat hand or the forearm. It was a wild and wonderful time, even in Soviet Russia, still artistically unfettered, still culturally a part of Europe. Even the great eclectic Hungarian master, Bartók, who absorbed elements that suited him from practically all these divergent styles and experiments and fused them into his own absolutely personal idiom, produced during the nineteen-twenties his most "difficult" works: the Second Violin Sonata, the First Piano Concerto, the Third String Quartet.

It was all very exciting for the keen young musician, but at no previous period in musical history had the composers—other than the timid and the reactionary, who were *ipso facto* of less consequence—got so far out of touch with the general musical public, the public for which they were supposed to be writing and which ought to have been listening to them. And this loss of touch, in every country of the cultural world, was equally bad for both parties. Something had to be done to bridge the gap—the first edition of this little book was an extremely modest attempt to help to bridge it, by bringing the public a little closer to the composers—and, as it happened, factors from a world that ought to be far removed from that of music began to play a part. First of all in Soviet Russia, with the launching of the first Five-Year Plan in 1929, came the official demand—not to be lightly ignored or evaded in a land where everything (including publishing) is state-controlled—for artists of every kind to collaborate in the furtherance of Government policy; and in 1932 that policy so far as it concerned writers and artists was described as one of "Soviet realism." Art must be for the people, comprehensible to the general public, not only to trained connoisseurs; it must reflect popular life and at the same time give that life the right direction by being virile and optimistic, never morbid or introspective. (There was, therefore, no question of a return to romanticism.) But it has not been easy for such gifted composers as Shostakovich to stifle their natural tendencies, simplify their utterance, and write in a style comprehensible and pleasing to Government officials; lacking a clear, definite standard of "Soviet realism," composers have again and again conceived themselves to be delivering the goods ordered and have been highly praised by Soviet critics for doing so, only to be sharply censured when unlucky chance has brought the compositions in question to the direct notice of some highly placed official with undeveloped or conservative musical tastes.

From 1933 onward the Nazi regime in Germany banned as "cultural Bolshevism" the very same type of music which the Bolshevists themselves banned as "bourgeois." Both regimes would have agreed that it was "decadent." The only difference was that the Russian composers had to stay at home and work out an acceptable compromise while the Germans—some of them good Aryans, like Hindemith—were able to find refuge abroad. America in particular became a great Ark of refuge for European composers fleeing from persecution and war.

All the same, these political pressures against extreme modernism only reinforced and hastened a natural tendency. We have only to notice the trends in other countries, where creative artists were free from official interference, to recognize that the tide had begun to turn early in the nineteen-thirties. A period of experimentation and transition in art is usually followed by one of consolidation and more permanent achievement. Some of the experiments of the nineteen-twenties were seen to have been futile—the quarter-tone experiment, for instance; others began to be accepted more generally as normal components of the modern idiom. A mellowing tendency became noticeable everywhere; musicians generally seemed to feel less self-conscious. Stravinsky's *Persephone* and Hindemith's *Mathis der Maler* in 1934, Berg's Violin Concerto and Bartók's Fifth Quartet in 1936, all reveal their composers in this mellower mood. Bartók's work in particular—the Violin Concerto of 1938 and the Sixth Quartet of 1939—shows how a real master may in the ease of his maturity draw nearer to the public without making concessions to it. The typical young English composer who was emerging into general public notice just before the Second World War and who has claimed a great deal of the world's limelight since, Benjamin Britten, is very far from being a revolutionary or "advanced." Like Bartók, he is an eclectic who has learned from all the modern schools and blended their teaching into an idiom of his own; but it is noteworthy that Britten (who was born in 1913) has evolved an idiom far less "difficult" in most respects than that of Bartók (who was born in 1881).

Even the rigid structure of twelve-tone music underwent a certain mellowing not only in the hands of Alban Berg but in Schoenberg's own. And, as we saw in the previous chapter, an American composer like Samuel Barber will now use it, not completely and consistently, but as a single element in his musical vocabulary.

EXAMPLE 33

a. 1923

With joyous movement (♩ = 108-112)

Sieh,— der Gott der ü - ber Völ - kern grollt—

- te, macht sich mild

(Schotts Söhne, Mainz)

One very interesting symptom of this desire of composers to simplify their utterance is the revision of early scores undertaken in recent years by such outstanding masters as Stravinsky and Hindemith. In 1946 * Stravinsky made a complete revision of his *Petrushka*, the original version of which dates from 1911. There is little change in the substance of the music, in its actual sound; but its appearance on paper is much simplified. It is much easier to read the new score; fussy details of orchestration and constant changes of time-signature are eliminated. Compare—to take an instance at ran-

* Not 1947, as marked on the cover of the new score.

EXAMPLE 33

Sieh, der Gott der ü - ber Völ - kern groll - te

macht sich mild ____ und kommt

(*Schotts Söhne, Mainz*)

dom—pages 70-71 of the old miniature score (Edition Russe de Musique) with pages 66–67 of the new (Boosey & Hawkes); the complication of the original version is shown to have been to some extent unnecessary, a false complication.

Similarly in 1947 Hindemith made an even more drastically changed new version of four numbers from *Das Marienleben*, a song-cycle for soprano and piano, originally composed in 1924. It will suffice to quote a passage from the seventh song, "Geburt Christi," in both versions (above and p. 130).

This is no mere change of orthography; the actual

sound of the music has been made easier to the ear. And of course this milder attitude of the contemporary composer during the last ten or fifteen years is not simply a weakening in the face of public opinion, a making of concessions in a spirit akin to political "appeasement"—though no doubt the pressure of public opinion has played a part in influencing some of our less distinguished contemporaries. It is mainly, as I have said above, the result of the working of a natural law of aesthetic history. And the taming of extreme dissonance and extreme rhythmic complication is also the outward manifestation of a change of spirit. The typical music of the nineteen-forties and early nineteen-fifties is still essentially an art of sound-structure, not of emotional expression. But emotion is no longer rigorously suppressed as in so much of the music written during the first fifteen years or so after the First World War. Its presence is allowed to be felt, sometimes deeply felt; but it is not allowed to gush freely, nor are composers any longer interested in dissecting it and revealing its subtle facets and fascinating perversions. It is frequently masked in some ironic way. There is no return to the romantic point of view, but composers no longer have to resist it self-consciously and defiantly. They are now no more afraid of emotion than Bach was, or Handel or Haydn or Mozart.

INDEX

-C 133 ⋺-

INDEX